The Value of Practical Knowledge

WISDOM of CHINA

Lily Mei

ISBN
978-1-957895-62-8 (Paperback)
978-1-957895-63-5 (eBook)

CONTENTS

PREFACE

I thought about writing this book for a long time. Yet, I put it off for various reasons. Then I remembered a statement from a very prominent Chinese philosopher, "A journey of a thousand miles begins with a single step." This statement really inspired me. Yes, I must begin my writing journey now. No matter how long it may take to complete, as long as I never stop, I will certainly reach my destination. I began my journey. The book of my heart, *Wisdom of China,* was born.

The history of China is extremely rich and profound. Throughout its long history, there have existed many dynasties, and each dynasty recorded numerous proverbs. The proverbs in this book provide a detailed cross-section of important proverbs from various dynasties. These proverbs exhibit the accumulated wisdom of Chinese people in an interesting and comprehensive manner.

Wisdom is called zhi hui 智慧 in Chinese language. The characters 智慧 indicate knowledge and brightness in your heart. Wisdom is much more valuable than wealth, and there is nothing in the world can compare with wisdom. If you seek after wisdom persistently, you will find her.

Let us consider an example of wisdom from history. King Solomon was the wisest king who ever lived. The following passage from 2 Chronicles 1:12 of the Bible shows that God provided King Solomon with wisdom, wealth, and honor. "Wisdom and knowledge are granted to you; and I will give you riches and wealth and honor, such as none of the kings have had who were before you, nor shall any after you have the like." Based on the passage, we can see that wisdom originates from God.

The fact that God is the source of wisdom means that wisdom is universal. For this reason, I believe that every nation possesses unique wisdom. I wrote this book because I wanted to share Chinese wisdom with you. It is absolutely unique and interesting. Wisdom allows us to make correct decisions and it furthermore prompts us to take required actions.

You and I perhaps will not meet face to face; however, you may be able to understand me when you read this book because it represents my heart. Because my heart is here, I hope I can truly speak to you through this book.

If I have actually accomplished that, then we can bond together via this book. You will know me; I also will know you. We become friends in the sense that we share and appreciate the same knowledge.

Before I put my pen down, I would like to tell you about myself. I was born into a very ordinary Chinese family. While I was growing up, I heard many of the Chinese proverbs which I wrote in this book. Many of the proverbs selected in this book are very dear to my heart, because I meditate upon them often. Wisdom can provide us with correct choices and can significantly strengthen our confidence. Chinese proverbs are very helpful guide to me, and I would like to express my heartfelt hope that you will appreciate them and find them helpful as well.

CHAPTER 1

Confidence

Chinese proverb: an ru tai shan.

安如泰山。

Translation: It is as secure as Mount Taishan.

Meaning: Be confident.

Application: Mount Taishan is one of five famous mountains in china. This mountain is very popular because it is magnificent and enormous, and it has been exposed to all sorts of turbulent weather for many generations. Today Mount Taishan stands as tall and strong as ever. Therefore, this proverb uses mount Taishan's unchanging strength, and steadiness to demonstrate confidence.

When a terrible storm arrives in our life, we must remain confident. The storm will eventually disappear, and the sun will shine for us again. The following story is related to this proverb.

My husband was going to lose his job as a software engineer. To lose a job is very unpleasant, and therefore my husband's heart was extremely heavy. Without a steady income, he would lose his house, his car, and everything else. What should he do with his crisis?

A person can be either totally panic or maintain confidence within. My husband chose the latter. He took immediate actions after receiving the terrible news. The first action was to tell all of his friends and family members to pray for him. The second action was to actively look for a new job. He relied on God to give him confidence and lift his burdens. God soon answered the prayers and provided a new job for him.

Chinese proverb: ji feng zhi jing cao.

疾风知劲草

Translation: The vigor of the grass is tested by a strong gale.

Meaning: How strong is one's confidence?

Application: A tempestuous wind tests the strength of the grass. After a severe windstorm disappears, and the grass is still standing healthy and tall, then the grass passed its test. In other words, that grass is super sturdy.

The severe windstorm represents trials or challenges, and the grass signifies a person. The tough challenges can test your confidence and strength. You will be just like the super sturdy grass described above if you determine to remain confident and pass the test.

Chinese proverb: sai weng shi ma, an zhi fei fu.

塞翁失马, 安知非福。

Translation: It may not be a misfortune when an old man loses his mare.

Meaning: A loss may turn out to be a gain.

Application: This proverb comes from a very popular story. According to a Chinese legend, an old man named Sai Weng lost his valuable mare one day. It was almost unthinkable to lose a mare, particularly for an aged person. Sai Weng went through tremendous effort to look for his precious possession, however, he could not find his mare. Sai Weng thought that his mare was gone for good, and he felt so miserable that he could not even eat.

While the man was still thinking gloomily about his lost mare, to his total surprise, the mare suddenly returned! The mare did not just return to the owner alone but also brought another horse with him. When Sai Weng gazed at two valuable horses, he could hardly believe his own eyes, and his heart immediately burst with joy!

The application of this proverb is that you may encounter a brief setback; nevertheless, you must never lose heart. When you come across a shocking blow, regardless of how dreadful the situation seems on the surface, you must always be hopeful and confident. Who can guess your temporary misery will bring you a long-term blessing?

Chinese proverb: shan chong shui fu yi wu lu, liu an hua ming you yi cun.

山重水复疑无路，柳暗花明又一村。

Translation: One may doubt there is a path in the midst of mountains and waterfalls; yet green willows and fresh flowers may open up a brand-new village.

Meaning: Look into a new beginning.

Application: The ancient Chinese used this proverb to portray the season of spring. For Chinese people, the spring season is the beginning of a new lunar year; therefore, they can always look into a new beginning. This proverb uses spring views of mountains, waters falls, green willows and fresh flowers to signify hope.

My mother once told me, "Without hope, people may perish. Without confidence, people may not accomplish. When people's hearts are filled with hope and confidence, they will be looking forward into a new beginning."

When I was a child, I saw a movie that I always remember. In the final scene of the movie, a general lost a very important battle and it was the end for him. He was completely depressed. When all hope seemed to be gone, a powerful friend arrived and spoke this proverb to him. The general was then able to look forward and realize that a new beginning was opening up for him.

When you are completely depressed and at your wits end, you need to renew your hope and confidence. The second half of this proverb, "green willows and fresh flowers may open up a brand-new village", implies that a brand-new world is patiently waiting for you.

Chinese proverb: sheng bai nai bing jia chang shi.

胜败乃兵家常事。

Translation: It is normal for the military to win or lose.

Meaning: Do not be too concerned about success or failure.

Application: This proverb tells us that military triumphs and defeats are very common. When two sides fight using their military strategies and forces, the result is usually the following: one side wins and the other side loses. Of course, there is no military in the whole world that desires to lose any battle because winning is everything. However, reality may force either triumph or defeat.

This proverb indicates that we need to hold onto a confident attitude and not let triumphs and failures in life sway us. Although winning or losing is important, in the long term, however, confidence is much more important. Confidence allows us to rise again and again from any defeats.

Chinese proverb: tian wu jue ren zhi lu.

天无绝人之路。

Translation: Heaven will not cut off a pathway for human beings.

Meaning: People always have hope.

Application: "Heaven will not cut off a pathway for human beings." This means that no matter how dreadful a situation may seem, there will always remain a path to get out. Therefore, we should never be in utter despair. Oh, how uplifting it is! We will always have hope; and hope produces comfort and confidence. For this reason, we shall always have peace in our hearts.

If we meditate just a little deeper, we will understand that these three elements of hope, comfort, and confidence are actually good friends and are interwoven. As long as we have breath, we can have hope! Along with hope, comfort and confidence will quietly dwell in our soul as well.

Chinese proverb: weng zhong zhuo bie.

瓮中捉鳖。

Translation: Grab a turtle in a pot.

Meaning: It is an easy task.

Application: Grabbing a turtle in a pot is an easy task. It is so easy that every person, young or old, can do it. It is pleasing to read a proverb which tells us that many things in this world are very easy. Our confidence is strengthened when we know that we have the capability to perform many tasks easily and well. Some of these easy tasks which spring into my mind in a minute include: cooking rice, encouraging children, and picking apples from an apple tree.

Chinese proverb: zhi ren zhe zhi, zi zhi zhe ming.

知人者智，自知者明。

Translation: To know people is wisdom, to know yourself is bright.

Meaning: We need to know both people and ourselves.

Application: This is simple yet very profound wisdom. It is of high importance to really understand people. We must try to truly understand the people with whom we have contact on a daily basis. A simple "hello-how are you" is not enough. Many people are hurting and need a sympathetic ear; others are lack friends and encouragement.

It does take effort to get to know others, however, it is harder to accurately know ourselves. If we really want to know ourselves, then we have to humble ourselves enough to critically understand and examine our desires, fears, loves, and motives. To truly understand ourselves allows us to live life more fully and be a bright light to others.

CHAPTER 2

Determination

Chinese proverb: bu dao huang he xin bu si.

不到黄河心不死。

Translation: One can never be stopped until one reaches the Yellow River.

Meaning: Never give up.

Application: The Yellow River is a powerful and extremely long river. According to Chinese history, the region around the Yellow River along with several other rivers formed the cradle of Chinese civilization. The Yellow River is very significant to Chinese citizens; the river is a subject of many Chinese songs such as the musical symphony "Ode to Yellow River".

"One can never be stopped until one reaches the Yellow River" tells us that we must have determination and perseverance. There is a universal need for people to hold onto an unbreakable spirit. The purpose of this proverb, therefore, is to offer encouragement to all. It is saying that people must cling to their strength of mind no matter what.

Suppose you have decided to do something, and you are truly convinced that it is the right thing to do. Friends, family and others around you may try to persuade you not to proceed. What should you do? Should you give up? No, you must never allow anyone to shake your spirit and determination. You should never give up your dreams and lifelong ambitions until you reach your Yellow River.

Chinese proverb: chong zheng qi gu.

重整旗鼓。

Translation: Rally one's force.

Meaning: It is time to start over again.

Application: "Rally one's force" is a proverb with a military application. This proverb can also be used in non-military situations. As a military proverb, it refers to a historic battle which was lost. Although a battle was lost, the war was not lost and the time to "Rally one's force" was at hand.

You may wonder how can you apply the principle of this proverb, and what does it take for a person to start over again? The following story can provide the answer.

A person desired to become a restaurant owner. He planned and carefully carried out the steps needed to fulfill his dream. Nevertheless, due to lack of experience, this person's first attempt was not successful. Learning from his mistakes, he knew what to do the second time around. Everything was going very well until, unfortunately, the economy of the land began to deteriorate. Quite a few businesses had to close their doors, and this particular restaurant was not immune from the downward spiral of the local economy; it had to close its doors as well.

To fail twice was a tremendous blow. To make matters worse, during the second failure, this man exhausted all of his finances. It was time to quit, he thought. However, deep down in his heart, he did not really want to give up. After the local economy recovered, the man decided to try for the third time. Finally, the third battle was a triumph!

The story, in general, can validate the true spirit of men and women their determination, persistence, and consistency. One man's business failure and eventual success may very well represent the true spirit which God placed in the heart of men and women.

Chinese proverb: jin shi wei kai.

金石为开。

Translation: One opens up a huge hard stone.

Meaning: A person determines to take up a tough challenge.

Application: According to a manuscript from the Han dynasty, a very interesting event occurred in the earlier Zhou dynasty. The manuscript contained the following: During the Zhou dynasty, there existed a very famous archer. The archer came from the state of Chu, and his name was Xiong Quzi. One night, the archer needed to pass through a mountainous region. Due to the darkness of the night, Xiong Quzi misidentified a huge rock as a tiger. For the sake of his physical safety, Xiong Quzi immediately took out his arrow and shot the "tiger" with all of his strength. After delivering his arrow, he went closer to look at the "tiger". When he looked at what he just shot, Xiong Quzi found out that the "tiger" was actually a huge tough rock. He was even more surprised to see that his arrow pierced through the huge rock. The news of Xiong Quzi shooting the "tiger" spread far and wide. People believed that the tough rock opened up for Xiong Quzi due to his determination.

Today, Chinese people use this proverb for opening up human's tough hearts. If we determine to touch people's hearts, we will be able to do so by being truly sincere. People will open their tough hearts to us when they see our genuine heart.

Chinese proverb: pai chu wan nan.

排除万难。

Translation: Surmount ten thousand difficulties.

Meaning: Overcome all obstacles.

Application: Is it possible for us to overcome all obstacles? The answer is yes, however, it is very difficult and requires strong determination.

When I consider difficulties which I have had to overcome in my life, I think of how overcoming each trial has strengthened me and enhanced my appreciation for life. My family lost nearly everything in the revolution following the second world war. We also had a very tough time during the Cultural Revolution. Jobs were granted by authorities. My father's monthly wage could only support himself; my mother's salary was purposely cut to a third by her employer. Difficulties gave us many hurdles to overcome and caused our family to work together in close and special ways.

Actually, difficulties are a part of life and no one is immune to them. Every individual struggles! As we go through life, it is helpful for us to know that we are not alone in having to overcome difficulties.

I believe that obstacles make life both challenging and interesting, and they may add some sparks in our life. Knowing that we all have trials and we all need to overcome them gives us great relief. We must be courageous and surmount our ten thousand difficulties one by one.

Chinese proverb: yi bu zuo, er bu xiu.

一不做,二不休。

Translation: Either do nothing or never rest.

Meaning: Do nothing or do everything needed.

Application: What does this proverb really imply? It implies firm determination. Firm determination indicates that people must never falter. The following two examples help to make the meaning of the proverb clear.

First example: Suppose a close friend of yours plans to invest in a real estate opportunity, and he would like you to join him. After carefully thinking it over, you decide not to join him. Because of this decision, you will do absolutely nothing. This is exactly what the first half of this proverb teaches.

Second example: Suppose your sister needed to have an operation, and she asked you to loan her the money. Even though you knew she might not be able to pay you back, you decided to help her. After you have made the decision to help her, you must never rest until you complete your commitment. This is the principle of the second half of the proverb "never rest".

Chinese proverb: you zhi zhe, shi jin cheng.

有志者，事竟成。

Translation: If you have determination, you will be a great achiever.

Meaning: You can become an accomplished person.

Application: Chinese proverbs should not be read just for fun. They should be studied and taken seriously. When we approach the proverbs in this way, they can inspire us. This proverb in particular can both inspire us and spur us on to greatness.

Determination is the key here. We must employ stubborn determination if we are to achieve our dreams and desires. If we are determined and endure, we will have great success.

My older son, David, can be used as an example here. When he was six years old, I told him the story of how my mother came from China when he was born to help take care of him as a baby. Unfortunately, it was winter and there was a sheet of ice on the driveway. My mother fell and broke her hip. I told David how my mother loved him and how a good doctor helped my mother with her hip. Ever since that day, my son wanted to become a doctor.

Over the years, this determination to be a doctor did not fade. In grade school and high school, David's preferences were toward science as this would move him closer to the goal. In college, he was well rounded but persisted in his dream. He was admitted to medical school and did very well. He is now a full-fledged doctor.

If you have a goal which you greatly desire, you can achieve this goal. The secret is to attain the goal and set in your mind and spirit a firm determination to succeed. Do not let the opinions of others or circumstances dissuade you. Yes, it will be difficult, and you will have setbacks.

Focus on your goal and let that goal motivate your actions. Persistently remind yourself to give your best effort every day. Do not let go of your dream. Go forward and be a great achiever.

Chinese proverb: zhi yao gong fu shen, tie chu mo cheng zhen.

只要功夫深, 铁杵磨成针。

Translation: Grinding an iron rod constantly will eventually turn it into a needle.

Meaning: One must be persistent and consistent.

Application: With persistency and consistency, people can move mountains. This proverb uses an iron rod and a spirit of endurance to express this truth. Although you may not grind an iron rod into a needle, you should be able to relate to this type of hard work and determination in your life.

The hard work and determination in your life might be your education. It might be building a business, or it could be something entirely different. As an example, if your desire is to become a doctor, you will know that the path is quite long and difficult. Nevertheless, if you are persistent and consistent, your iron rod (studying medicine in this case) will someday become the needle you desire. The needle, in this case, will be your accomplishment of becoming a medical doctor.

CHAPTER 3

Education

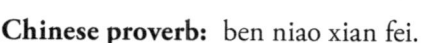

Chinese proverb: ben niao xian fei.

笨鸟先飞。

Translation: A clumsy bird flies early.

Meaning: Slow learners need to start first.

Application: "A clumsy bird flies early" is a metaphor, and it is often applied in education. The proverb suggests that if a bird is slower than other birds, then this bird needs to start flying ahead of the rest of birds. By flying first, this bird then will not fall behind.

In Chinese culture, people frequently use this proverb to describe themselves as clumsy birds or slow learners. However, they may not actually be slow learners at all. There are two common reasons that Chinese people consider themselves "slow." The number one reason is that they just want to get ahead by starting early. This indicates an eagerness to learn. The second reason Chinese people describe themselves as clumsy birds is that they are being modest. In Chinese culture, a person using either of these reasons is considered to have a good attitude toward learning.

Chinese proverb: bo xue duo cai.

博学多才。

Translation: One is a learned scholar with exceptional skills.

Meaning: A person is erudite and gifted.

Application: Chinese people, in general, give high esteem to individuals who are erudite and gifted. Esteem for scholarly and talented individuals has been in place since the beginning of Chinese civilization. Admiration for intellectual and well-educated individuals is deeply inscribed within Chinese people's hearts, and this is unlikely to ever change. If you wish to be treated with high esteem, devote yourself to attaining quality education.

Chinese proverb: bu chi xia wen.

不耻下问。

Translation: There is no shame in asking subordinates for knowledge.

Meaning: Acquiring knowledge should bear no humiliation.

Application: No one should feel embarrassed to ask questions and seek knowledge, whether the knowledge comes from a superior or a subordinate. This proverb specifically references asking subordinates for knowledge. These subordinates can include a variety of individuals. They may be people who work for you, people who have less education than you, are younger than you, etc.

I have a friend who would be a good example of this type of person. This friend never attended college and yet he has deep knowledge in many subjects. He is an expert regarding automobile related knowledge. Some people would call this person a car doctor. He can diagnose and correct a wide variety of problems with vehicles. When friends of this man have vehicle difficulties, they know whom they should inquire for knowledge.

Chinese proverb: bu xue wu shu.

不学无术。

Translation: One possesses no skills if one cares not to learn.

Meaning: Education is very necessary.

Application: Every person needs education. If a person does not want to learn, then he or she will not develop needed skills. Skills are required to work and bring home a paycheck. The reality which this proverb conveys is that those who do not wish to learn will have great difficulties in life. A willingness to learn is important to all, however, it is particularly important for young people. If a young person desires to learn, that person will have a successful career and life; an unwillingness to learn in a young person will put that individual on the path to failure.

Chinese proverb: chi de ku zhong ku, fang wei ren shang ren.

吃得苦中苦，方为人上人。

Translation: By enduring the toughest hardship, one may become an extraordinary achiever.

Meaning: Without suffering, one may not become a superb individual.

Application: Diamonds are created from carbon under extreme pressure. In a similar way, extraordinary achievers are created by enduring the toughest hardship. What might be some examples of this "toughest hardship"? Rising from extreme poverty, overcoming a physical handicap or enduring oppression, etc. These and many other hardships will create the pressure to produce people who are like diamonds.

There was a mathematician in China who was put into prison. This man had been interested in solving an extremely complex mathematical problem. While he endured the hardships of prison, he became the first mathematician to find the solution for the problem.

Chinese proverb: du zhi hao xue.

笃志好学。

Translation: Devote one's mind to learning.

Meaning: Focus your mind and heart toward acquiring knowledge.

Application: Throughout Chinese history, scholars and those who pursue wisdom and knowledge have always been treated with esteem and high regard. A renowned example of one who devoted his life to acquiring and sharing knowledge is Confucius.

Confucius (551-479 BC) was not born into a privileged family. His father died when he was 3 years old. When Confucius was 15 years old, he set his heart on learning. He then focused his mind and heart toward acquiring knowledge and became the most learned man of his time. Confucius created schools where hundreds of students were trained. There was not distinction between rich or poor, and admittance to the schools was based on eagerness to learn. In China's long history, Confucius is considered as its greatest sage and philosopher.

This proverb urges all of us to devote our hearts and minds toward learning. It is because history reveals to us that devoting one's mind to studying has resulted in positive outcomes.

Chinese proverb: ku jin gan lai.

苦尽甘来。

Translation: Award comes after hard work.

Meaning: Hardship will end and then satisfaction will come.

Application: This proverb is a very encouraging statement. We can relate to this statement in several ways. Education, for instance, can be one of them. In general, a basic education takes 12 years. For people who wish to be professionals such as engineers or scientists, 16 years or longer may be required.

"Award comes after hard work", places the focus on the award, not the time. If you are a student and think that education takes too much of your time, you are not alone. But if you can stand the test of time, someday your long period of hard work will in due course bring you the sweet happiness of your accomplishment.

Chinese proverb: li zheng shang you.

力争上游。

Translation: Make great efforts to reach the top.

Meaning: Strive for the best.

Application: Chinese people are extremely competitive. This competitive spirit is very visible in the area of intellectual pursuits. Chinese parents teach their children from an early age to pursue academic and intellectual careers; they also urge them to achieve the best in their chosen field of expertise. "Make great efforts to reach the top" is the most often used motto in Chinese culture.

Chinese proverb: liang shi yi you.

Translation: Good teachers and helpful friends are beneficial.

良师益友。

Meaning: A favorable educational environment can help students to learn.

Application: This proverb points out two important components which are beneficial in learning, namely good teachers and helpful friends. Both of these should be sought by students and valued when found.

A good teacher is one who cares for students. Students can sense and will positively respond to a teacher who is knowledgeable, enthusiastic and caring. This type of teacher will bring out the best in students and will create an environment where learning is exciting and fun.

Helpful friends are of great value in learning. A good method of finding a helpful friend is to be a friend first. When a fellow student encountered learning difficulties, you should go out of your way to give help without looking for anything in return. It will be surprising to see that by being helpful, you soon will have friends to help you.

Chinese proverb: neng zhe wei shi.

能者为师。

Translation: Whoever possesses expertise can be a teacher.

Meaning: Knowledgeable people have subjects to teach.

Application: This proverb informs us every person can be a teacher if he or she has expertise and a willingness to share that expertise. This is not limited to those who have learned and prepared to teach subjects such as history or literature.

The "whoever" in this proverb can be anyone. For example, hairstylists can teach people how to cut hair, and tailors can teach people how to make clothes, etc. The reality is that virtually every individual on earth possesses a certain kind of knowledge and skills. However, knowledgeable people must be modest students first, and then they will know how to teach others.

Chinese proverb: qing chu yu lan er sheng yu lan.

青出于蓝而胜于蓝。

Translation: Indigo blue is bluer than the indigo plant.

Meaning: Students can surpass their teachers.

Application: Indigo blue is one of the colors of the rainbow. This particular blue color can be extracted from the indigo plant, and it is a very pretty color. Actually, the color is a prettier blue than the plant color.

What the Chinese really want to say is this: Students can surpass their teachers. They want to use this proverb to point out that great teachers may produce greater pupils than themselves, just as the created indigo blue becomes a better color than its original plant color.

In fact, history has recorded quite a few students who not only exceeded their teachers but also became exceptionally renowned. You perhaps have heard of Tchaikovsky.

Tchaikovsky was not only one of the Russia's most brilliant composers but was also one of the world's brilliant masters in music. Does anyone know who Tchaikovsky's teachers were? The answer may be nobody knows unless the person studies music history. However, almost everyone has heard of Tchaikovsky. This brilliant Russian composer absolutely surpassed his own teachers by far.

Chinese proverb: shen cang ruo xu.

深藏若虚。

Translation: Be modest about one's talent.

Meaning: Do not show off.

Application: Modesty is considered to be an important merit in Chinese culture. Therefore, Chinese people teach their children the value of modesty at a very early age. The following story is a fine example of this proverb being lived out.

A Chinese architect, along with other architects, designed a very famous building in China, and this building stands as a world-class structure today. After the architect completed the project, he came to the United States to live. Years later he wanted to take his family to visit China. Naturally, the architect also wanted to see the prominent building he had co-designed. Somehow, the news leaked out. The moment he and his family arrived at the building, a very grand welcome party greeted them. The architect was completely surprised, and he felt very embarrassed for the recognition.

The recognition totally surprised another person, and that person was none other than the architect's daughter. The daughter learned for the very first time that her father was extremely famous. She was also surprised that her father never mentioned to her that he co-designed the famous building. Being an intelligent child, she learned not just the truth about her father's fame but also a lesson about her father's modesty.

After they returned to America, the daughter told her nextdoor neighbor about her father's embarrassing episode. The neighbor was very surprised at not knowing that a distinguished architect lived next door.

Chinese proverb: tao li man tian xia.

桃李满天下。

Translation: Peaches and plums are all over the world.

Meaning: Educators have pupils everywhere.

Application: Peaches and plums are fruits, which most people enjoy eating. When peaches and plums are ripe, they fill the air with a sweet aroma. When you put a piece of ripe peach or plum into your mouth, you will be delighted with the delicious sweet taste. Farmers who cultivate these fruits enjoy seeing the results of their labor.

This proverb is a metaphor. It is a Chinese tradition that they use peaches and plumbs to indicate pupils; teachers are naturally the cultivators of their "peaches" and "plumbs". These pupils will be in many and varied careers, industries and places. When teachers learn of their student's successes, they will be delighted.

Chinese proverb: yan shi chu gao tu.

严师出高徒。

Translation: A strict teacher will produce quality pupils.

Meaning: Discipline produces good pupils.

Application: It takes hard and focused work to produce quality results. Students need to have positive work ethic to achieve success, and strict teaches are needed to help develop this ethic.

When we read biographies of famous individuals, we often find that they became well known is because they had strict teachers. According to this proverb, a strict teacher will produce quality pupils. Jaime Escalante can be used as one example in the following paragraph.

Jaime Escalante taught math during the mid 70s at the most underperforming school in Los Angeles—Garfield high school. Instead of passing his students with easy math, he challenged them with higher math. His strict, drill-sergeant style faced resistance from the student body and the administration. His approach, however, eventually began to show positive results. In 1988, Jaime Escalante was awarded the Presidential Medal for Excellence in Education.

Chinese proverb: yi cun guang yin yi cun jin, cun jin nan mai cun guang yin.

一寸光阴一寸金，寸金难买寸光阴。

Translation: An inch of time and an inch of gold, that inch of gold cannot buy that inch of time.

Meaning: Time is much more valuable than precious gold.

Application: People can produce precious gold by mining; however, none of us can ever produce time. Nobody can! Gold in this proverb implies earthly wealth. If we compare the importance of time with earthly wealth, time will always win!

Time is unquestionably priceless; therefore, the Chinese use this proverb to encourage young people to value their time and use as much time as possible for their education. Chinese people believe that if youngsters truly understand the value of time, they will devote their best time in life to learn and to make great achievements.

Chinese proverb: zhong ling yu xiu.

钟灵毓秀。

Translation: Concentrate on environment to make superb individuals.

Meaning: Right environment produces right people.

Application: After reading fifteen Chinese proverbs concerning education, you certainly understand its importance. Yes, Chinese people really place education at the top of their list. However, they believe that education alone is not enough. In addition to education, the Chinese also place emphasis on appropriate environment.

No doubt, an appropriate environment is especially important for children. Education and environment are the two essential components for children's upbringing. Because of that belief, many Chinese parents have tried to make the best effort to provide the right education and the right environment for their children. One of the main beliefs that Chinese parents firmly have confidence in is that if children grow up in an appropriate environment, they will become valuable citizens someday. Furthermore, they also believe that their efforts will generate fruitful results.

You perhaps have heard of a Chinese story called "Meng Mu San Qian". This story tells of a mother who changed her residence three times for the sake of her son. The reason for changing the residence was that the mother wanted her son to be nurtured in a suitable environment. The result of the mother's best efforts for her son was indeed rewarding; the mother was none other than Mencius' mother, and the son was Mencius (372-289 BC). Because Mencius grew up in a suitable surrounding, he eventually became a truly renowned individual—a prominent Chinese philosopher. Chinese people consider Mencius as the Second Sage, after Confucius himself.

When Mencius was a young boy, his father passed away, and his mother raised him alone. During that time, Mencius and his mother lived near a cemetery.

As a young child, Mencius and other children often played games together. The game they played was mimicking the grown-ups. Because of the fact that Mencius lived so close to the cemetery, he and other children imitated religious actions. Those actions included mourning rites and other related activities. When Mencius' mother saw the activities of her son, she felt very troubled. She believed that her son was not growing up in an appropriate environment. As a result, Mencius' mother decided to move.

Mencius and his mother moved to a place near a market. The market was a very busy place, and it was usually full of people. Mencius was curious about people; thus, he began to observe people in the busy market. He found out that butchers were interesting people, so he began to mimic the activities of butchers. Mencius' mother saw her child playing butcher's game regularly, she knew that they must move again.

This time, Mencius and his mother moved to a residence near a school. Being interested in the new environment, Mencius began to observe activities of the school. He observed how teachers and pupils respectfully treated each other. At the same time, he could hear the students' reading and reciting their textbooks. From then on, Mencius began to mimic the activities of teachers and students. When Mencius' mother saw her son behaved very politely, she was very satisfied. She knew that moving near the school was the right choice. Mencius' mother believed that her son would grow up to be a fine gentleman. In fact, Mencius became both a gentleman and a renowned sage.

CHAPTER 4

Happiness

Chinese proverb: an pin le dao.

安贫乐道。

Translation: One should have peace and joy even in poverty.

Meaning: Money cannot buy peace and happiness.

Application: Most people in this world want to become wealthy. This is because people believe that wealth can solve all kinds of problems. In addition to that, they think money can purchase their happiness.

You may be one of those people who want to become wealthy. You are very certain of yourself that you can be very happy if you have plenty of material goods. The idea is not wrong at all. Rich people can obtain what they please. However, if you compare genuine happiness with owning abundant material things, the two are not necessary the same. Wealth surely can purchase material goods; however, it can never purchase true happiness. Actually, some wealthy people are quite miserable. You will read in the following about one of the wealthiest individuals of the world during a specified period.

J. Paul Getty (1892-1976), a billionaire, was the founder of the Getty Oil Company. At his death, he left more than two billion-dollar worth of wealth. While Paul Getty was alive, one of his grandsons was kidnapped. When the kidnappers asked for a ransom of seventeen million dollars, Paul Getty refused to pay the ransom. As a result, his grandson lost one of his ears. You can find similar stories about extremely wealthy individuals. Truly, money cannot buy peace and happiness.

My mother lived a life of both prosperity and poverty. She was born into a wealthy family, however, due to events associated with the Chinese civil war and the second world war, she became very poor. Whether she was rich or poor, my mother's heart was filled with peace and joy. She often mentioned to me a very popular Chinese proverb, **"知足者，常乐也"**. This proverb indicates that if a person is truly content, then this person will live a joyous life. I believe that exact proverb was my mother's life-long motto. Because of her contentment with whatever she had, along with her appropriate outlook on life, my mother lived a long life.

Chinese proverb: an ju le ye.

安居乐业。

Translation: One should live in peace and take pleasure in one's own work.

Meaning: People should dwell in tranquility and enjoy what they do.

Application: This proverb provides a very sound recommendation to all people; it is that we should live in peace and take pleasure in our own work. To live in peace and to enjoy our work are two very simple basics. Indeed, a pleasant human life requires peace and enjoyment.

When people live a peaceful life and enjoy their livelihood, they can attain many benefits. Some of the benefits include better physical and psychological health. This is because real treasure of our life is not money. Real treasure is derived from contentment in life.

Chinese proverb: bai zi hui tou jin bu huan.

败子回头金不换。

Translation: The return of the prodigal is worth much more than gold.

Meaning: The value of a changed person is measureless.

Application: If you once were a prodigal son or a daughter, you knew how much pain you had generated for your parents. The pain was beyond any language in this world could express. Then you changed! You returned to become an ethical individual. When that took place, the joy you gave to your parents was extraordinarily delightful.

As this proverb states, "The return of the prodigal is worth much more than gold." It is absolutely true! Your returning is worth more to your parents than all the gold in the whole world.

Chinese proverb: fu ru dong hai.

福如东海

Translation: May you be blessed like East China Sea.

Meaning: It is an abundant blessing.

Application: The best character in Chinese language perhaps is the first character of this proverb. Of course, this is just my humble opinion. Every time I see the character, "福—blessing", my heart will be overflowing with joy. In other words, I have special pleasant feelings toward what I consider to be the best character in Chinese language. Let us now consider the remaining characters of this proverb. The second character means like, and the last two characters designate "East China Sea".

Therefore, this proverb states that "May you be blessed like East China Sea." The East China Sea is enormous, and it will never run out of water. If blessings are flowing like the sea, then you will receive perpetual blessings and be very delighted. From our discussion, you can conclude that this proverb gives people a sense of great joy.

Chinese proverb: ji ren tian xiang.

吉人天相。

Translation: Auspicious people get extra blessings and protections from heaven.

Meaning: The heaven looks after its favorable individuals.

Application: All of us in this world receive blessings and protections. According to Chinese philosophy, there are individuals who can receive extra favors from heaven. Those who receive extra favors are auspicious people, and auspicious individuals are predestined to obtain special blessings and protections.

You may have observed some things regarding others during your life which show the truth of this proverb. These things might be difficult to believe, and you cannot find logical explanations. Some individuals try very hard all of their lives, and yet they receive very little; other people may try very little or not try at all, and yet they obtain a lot. How can that be?

The reality is that some individuals, who get little, are not auspicious people. The other people, who try very little and receive plenty, are the auspicious people. Auspicious people, in the eyes of the heaven, are extra special. They receive particular blessings and protections from above.

In life we all encounter various trials and challenges; however, if you are an auspicious person, then you should be exceptionally joyful and grateful. You can rely on heaven, and you do not need to worry. Based on this proverb, heaven will look after you in a very specific way. You can live at ease with predetermined blessings and protections.

Chinese proverb: man mian chun feng.

满面春风。

Translation: A person's whole face is full of spring breeze.

Meaning: A content person has a pleasant mood.

Application: This proverb portrays a satisfied expression on a person's face. In general, if people are truly happy, they usually show it on their faces. When a person is full of joy and has inner pleasant feelings, that joy is not easily hidden, it will be displayed on their faces. When your whole face is full of spring breeze, it indicates that you are in a very pleasant mood.

My first child is a girl. After eighteen hours of long and difficult labor, a baby was born and my doctor told me, "It's a girl!" My heart immediately burst with joy! Wow! A girl! Although my physical body was in pain, my heart was happy, and my face was full of spring breeze. A few days later, my mother called me over the phone from China, she said that I needed to take very good care of my new daughter. She believed that someday my girl would be a good helper to me. My mother's words have proven to be true.

Chinese proverb: xin hua nu fang.

心花怒放。

Translation: Heart blooms like a flower with exceeding joy.

Meaning: One is exceptionally happy.

Application: One of my cousins grew up in the United States; therefore, she could not read Chinese characters. During one of our conversations, she told me that she could distinguish differences between happy characters and unhappy characters. Other people also told me the same thing once or twice. Some foreigners who do not know the Chinese language can recognize characters representing joy, anger, grief and pleasure. The explanation for this phenomenon may be that the Chinese language was created in an incredibly complex and marvelous way.

If you are one of the individuals mentioned above who can discern distinctions between the characters, then you may say this proverb contains the happy characters. The first two characters of this proverb stand for flowers in the heart; the last two characters indicate wildly open or burst completely. You know that human eyes cannot see flowers in people's heart, even though they may intangibly exist.

This proverb refers to extremely happy people. What can make an individual extremely happy? This question is very difficult to answer. It is because there are many kinds of individuals in the world; therefore, it all depends on the people and circumstances. Some people could be extremely happy due to an ideal promotion while other people's heart might bloom completely because of they are starting a new life. When your heart blooms like a flower with exceeding joy, you know precisely why.

Chinese proverb: zhi zhu zhe, chang le ye.

知足者，常乐也。

Translation: True happiness comes from contentment.

Meaning: Content people are happy people.

Application: This is a very straightforward proverb. It states that true happiness comes from contentment of the human heart. Therefore, if you desire authentic happiness, then you need to be content. If you look around, you will find that truly content people are happy people. Moreover, those content people may not necessary possess much wealth, yet they are happy. How can they be happy? It is because genuine happiness is not from without but is from within.

Some people may not believe that people who without much wealth can be happy. They may ask, "Is it true that genuine happiness comes from within?" The answer is yes. People can certainly enjoy their life without much wealth.

Now let us delve into the subject of wealth a little further. An indisputable fact is that the world's wealth is not equally distributed. There exist exceptionally rich people and extremely poor people in the world. Regardless of rich or poor, people should be very content with whatever they possess.

We can move toward contentment by understanding that not everything must be perfect. The unequally distributed wealth system is not something that we can fix. Then should you complain or accept reality? You know the answer. Attempting to change reality by complaining is nearly hopeless and does not lead to contentment.

Medical studies show that a person's physical health is closely related to their psychological health. Having stress and agony in your heart will eventually cause physical illness. Based on what we have reviewed, the lack or abundance of money should not affect contentment. If you learn to appreciate and be satisfied with what you possess, then you will be a happy person.

Chinese proverb: zhuan huo wei fu.

转祸为福。

Translation: Turn calamities into blessings.

Meaning: Adversities may be altered.

Application: Chinese people believe the traditional saying of **祸兮福所倚, 福兮祸所伏**. This saying can be translated as "Good fortune lies within bad, bad fortune lurks within good." According to this belief, calamities might transform into blessings. If you yourself have experienced adversities changed to become good fortunes, then you will unquestionably agree with this proverb. However, if you disagree with the above statement, then I would like to tell you a true story related to "Adversities may be altered".

Once upon a time, there was a village where the villagers lived their lives in peace. Then a war erupted in the land and the peace in that village disappeared. Worse yet, the villagers were in constant danger of Japanese invaders. During that particular period, there was a lovely pregnant woman who lived in the village.

One day, some villagers saw that a group of Japanese invaders was approaching their village. Therefore, they told everyone to escape right away. All of the people in that village escaped very quickly. The whole village was empty except for that one pregnant woman. Because the pregnant woman was very near to her delivery date, and she had learned the news of the invaders late, the woman could not escape in time.

When the woman saw the invaders approaching her front yard, she was horrified, and her panic almost made her paralyzed. Suddenly an idea came into her mind so she immediately acted. The pregnant woman hid herself at one corner on her bed with half of the mosquito net down. A few minutes later, the invaders stepped into her bedroom and looked around hastily. They then left. What a narrow escape! The pregnant woman thought about her life and death moment. And not too long after that incident, the woman gave a birth to her first baby.

It would be a total tragedy if the invaders had found her that day! Actually, that lovely pregnant woman was my mother, and that baby, which my mother delivered soon after the narrow escape, is my older sister. My sister today is a retired educator and a grandmother.

This story is just one of many stories of adversities averted or turned into blessings in real life. The traditional Chinese saying of "good fortune lies within bad, bad fortune lurks within good" has been proven more than once in my family. Chinese history has recorded numerous calamities turned into blessings.

CHAPTER 5

Leadership

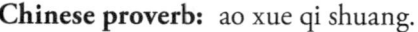

Chinese proverb: ao xue qi shuang.

傲雪欺霜。

Translation: Do not be afraid of snow and frost.

Meaning: Refuse to yield to difficulties.

Application: This proverb begins the chapter on leadership by emphasizing an important quality of leaders. That quality is the ability to rise above and persevere through trials and difficulties. The snow and frost mentioned in the proverb indicate difficulties and problems which occur often in our lives. Good leaders understand that solving and overcoming problems is a large and important part of their job. Difficulties are constantly arriving, and leaders must not fear them, rather, they should work to anticipate and quickly resolve them.

We all know that winter comes every year, and we should welcome the snow and frost as a part of life. We may not all be in leadership roles; however, we will do well to have a resolute spirit and not be afraid of snow and frost.

Chinese proverb: bai bai bu zhe.

百败不折。

Translation: Failed a hundred times, and yet not give up.

Meaning: One has an unbreakable spirit.

Application: This proverb originated during the Song dynasty (AD 960-1279). Many events recorded in Chinese history and referenced in proverbs occurred during this dynasty which lasted a little over three hundred years. One event involved emperor Shang Xiao Zong and one of his officials. The emperor was very pleased with the official who had failed many times and yet did not give up. The emperor gave great praise to that official who had demonstrated an enduring spirit. The emperor made the following statement which this proverb repeats: "Failed a hundred times and still unbreakable. This is a man after my own heart."

Since the emperor was the highest leader of the nation, the statement was highly valued and became a great inspiration to all levels of leaders. All leaders, from the leader of a nation to the leader of a family, will have challenges and failures. Life cannot always be smooth sailing. All of us would do well to emulate that official from long ago who failed a hundred times and yet did not give up.

Chinese proverb: bing zai jing er bu zai duo.

兵在精而不在多。

Translation: A few refined soldiers are better than a lot of soldiers.

Meaning: Quality matters more than quantity.

Application: Even in warfare, quality is better than quantity. By reading war documentaries, you will learn that generals would rather have a smaller number of seasoned and well-trained soldiers than a larger number of inexperienced soldiers. Refined, well trained soldiers are leaders and experts. Leaders and experts are what it takes to get the job done. There is truth in the old saying, "Twenty percent of the people accomplish eighty percent of the work."

Although this proverb references military soldiers, the teaching of the proverb applies to ordinary people as well. You and I should strive to be a part of the twenty percent who are leaders and experts. Also, when we assemble a group of people to accomplish a job, we should choose quality over quantity.

Chinese proverb: bu pian bu yi.

不偏不倚。

Translation: One handles things fairly.

Meaning: A leader must be impartial.

Application: This proverb addresses impartiality. An impartial person can handle matters very fairly. If you take a moment to consider the above characters of this proverb, you then can understand the true meaning of fairness. The first two characters indicate not to incline to one side, and the last two characters point toward not to rely on only one opinion. To summarize the characters, one should be fair, impartial and willing to listen to more than one opinion. These qualities are particularly important to people who are in leadership positions.

Who are the people in leadership positions? You might well be one of them. There are leaders almost everywhere. At home, a parent is the leader. At school, a teacher is the leader of students; and the principal is the leader of teachers. At workplace, people with authority are the leaders. Also, people not in leadership roles who take initiative to solve problems are in fact leaders.

When a dispute occurs between two sides at home, at school, or in the workplace, the leader must solve the dispute in an impartial manner not inclining to one side or relying on only one opinion. When the impartial leader solves conflicts very reasonably, then every side can receive a fair treatment.

Chinese proverb: cong zhe ru yun.

从者如云。

Translation: Have followers like the clouds.

Meaning: A dynamic leader can attract a multitude.

Application: The first two characters of this proverb indicate "followers"; the last two characters mean "clouds". Clouds in the sky can gather and increase in number. The proverb therefore is used to describe a dynamic leader who can attract a multitude just as a magnet can attract iron.

A person who can draw a huge multitude possesses incredible influence. When a dynamic leader has vision and has followers like the clouds, he can accomplish great things.

Chinese proverb: dan lue jian ren.

胆略兼人。

Translation: A person's courage and ingenuity surpass others.

Meaning: An individual has superior qualities.

Application: This proverb describes qualities of superior individuals. What can make an individual be superior? Based on this proverb, a superior person not only possesses courage and ingenuity but also surpasses courage and ingenuity of other people.

Is it right? Yes, it is right. The third character of this proverb, 兼, indicates greater than ordinary. In other words, a superior individual must have greater courage and ingenuity than the rest of the people. Leaders are expected to outshine the people they lead; therefore, individuals who possess superior qualities should be leaders.

Chinese proverb: guan guan xiang hu.

官官相护。

Translation: Officials protect each other mutually.

Meaning: Officials are partial to one another.

Application: Officials are leaders, however, like ordinary citizens, they often need help. When they need help, they must rely on other officials. If officials do not protect each other, then who else will shield them? Officials are therefore obliged to mutually protect each other. Let us now analyze this proverb from two different perspectives.

First, let us assume you are an authorized official. Being an officer, you will be partial to other officers. Why? The reason is quite simple. It is because you are one of them and thus you are inclined to help. When you need assistance, other officials will come to support you as well. As an official, the truth that officials protect each other works well for you.

Now let us flip the coin and suppose that you are not in charge. You have just gotten in a conflict with you supervisor. What should you do? Should you go to another leader and complain? No, you should not. According to this proverb, supervisors protect each other mutually. It would do you more harm than good if you complain to another leader. To do so would put you into a double jeopardy situation. First of all, it is very likely you would not get any sympathy from the other leader. Also, you might receive retaliation from your direct supervisor and put future promotions in jeopardy. For all of the reasons listed, you should do the right thing. The right thing is, if you desire to keep the job, to reconcile with your boss. Reconciliation is not only the correct action but also is the most feasible option.

Chinese proverb: hao yan zhuang yu.

豪言壮语。

Translation: One can utter grand and heroic words.

Meaning: Great speakers can persuade the audience.

Application: This proverb refers to those who have exceptional communication skills. Individuals who articulate remarkably well are born leaders. They can express their thoughts and feelings so exceptionally well that their grand and heroic vocabulary may completely persuade the audience. Leaders who possess natural charisma can arouse people and stimulate the atmosphere at important assemblies. When the common people's enthusiasm is set off, then the atmosphere of the assembly can really be stirred up.

Think of any major historical event and consider the circumstances. In most cases, the event was promoted or explained by extremely motivating speeches delivered by great orators using appealing words.

The First Crusade of 1095 is a very good example. One dynamic leader persuaded vast numbers of people to leave their homes and families and travel to a distant land. This dynamic leader was Pope Urban II. His November of 1095 speech at Clermont in southern France was exceptionally stimulating. It was so stimulating that it eventually made an unforgettable episode in history.

The historical record contains large numbers of remarkable communicators. It has been true in the past, it is true today and it will be true in the future. Outstanding leaders will continue to make history.

Chinese proverb: jian ting ze ming, pian xin ze an.

兼听则明，偏信则暗。

Translation: Listen to both sides, and one will be enlightened; heed only one side, and one will be benighted.

Meaning: Be a wise leader.

Application: Leaders of various levels often need to resolve conflicts; therefore, this proverb is most suited to leaders. When conflicts occur, leaders not only need to be fair minded but also need to have wisdom. According to this proverb, an enlightened leader will listen to both sides; a benighted leader heeds only one side.

If you would like to become a wise leader, you would do well to enhance your skill of listening to both sides. A wise leader will make great effort to be both impartial and understanding. Prior to making a judgment, it is very important for you to listen to all sides. In addition, you must also investigate and process all of the facts. You will then be in a position to weigh all considerations and resolve issues.

Chinese proverb: jing shang ai xia.

敬上爱下。

Translation: Honor those who are above you and be kind to those who are beneath you.

Meaning: Be respectful to your elders and leaders and be compassionate to those younger and beneath you.

Application: We should show respect to those who are older than us, and we should hold our leaders in high esteem. As for "compassionate", the right behavior is that we need to be kind to those who are younger than we are. If we have subordinates, we also need to show kindness to them. In a nutshell, this proverb teaches people to behave respectfully and kindly.

I have found that many successful and high-level leaders do show respect and kindness to others. The truth is people who respect others will also receive respect; people who have a compassionate heart will receive compassion. I think that wise leaders normally demonstrate gracious manners. Furthermore, being at the top, they can certainly obtain people's esteem.

Chinese proverb: kuai dao zhan luan ma.

快刀斩乱麻。

Translation: One cuts tangled hemp with a sharp knife.

Meaning: A person can come up with a quick solution.

Application: This proverb originated from the Northern dynasties. During the Eastern Wei Period (AD 534-550) of the Northern dynasties, a particular event was recorded. It was about a sharp-minded person who knew how to solve an issue very quickly.

According to the commentary, a prime minister named Gao Huan wanted to know each of his sons' intelligence. He then came up with an idea. One day, the prime minister brought a big bundle of tangled hemp. The prime minister wanted to use the tangled hemp as a method to test how intelligent each of his sons were. He first gave each son one bundle of tangled hemp, and then he told all of his sons that they needed to compete with each other to see who could untangle the hemp the fastest.

After he handed out the tangled hemp, the prime minister was very eager to see which son could put the tangled hemp in order first. All of his sons, except one, were carefully pulling one string after another. The only son who did not do what his brothers were doing left. Quickly, he returned with a very sharp knife. Then he started to chop the tangled hemp. Very soon, he chopped all of the tangled hemp in order. He was first.

Seeing this particular son untangle his hemp in such a short time, the prime minister was greatly delighted. He then asked the winner why he had used the knife to chop the hemp. The winner answered, "Whoever causes trouble must be cut down." The answer amazed the prime minister, and he believed that this son would have a promising future. The father's belief became reality. The winner of the tangled hemp competition eventually became an emperor.

Today, the Chinese use this proverb to teach leadership skills. This proverb teaches leaders that issues can be solved very speedily with a sharp mind. Without any doubt, bright leaders can come up with appropriate solutions quickly for different challenges and obstacles.

Chinese proverb: lei sheng da yu dian xia.

雷声大雨点小。

Translation: There are big thunders and yet only a few raindrops.

Meaning: There is hardly any action.

Application: You may know some people whose words and actions are not connected. They talk very big, yet they do not act according to their own words. This proverb provides an excellent description for those whose words do not match their deeds, "There are big thunders and yet only a few raindrops".

This proverb tries to teach people the principle of trust worthiness. People must be honest and do what they say. Otherwise, they could become hypocrites. Even though this proverb applies to every person, it is especially important to leaders. This is because leaders have followers watching them, and they need to have their words and deeds in unison.

Chinese proverb: shen zi di li.

深自砥砺。

Translation: Sharpen oneself diligently like whetting a knife.

Meaning: A person works hard with self-discipline.

Application: This proverb is based on commentaries of *Romance of the Three Kingdoms*. The following is a list of the three kingdoms:

Wei – 魏 (AD 220-265)

Shu – 蜀 (AD 221-263)

Wu – 吴 (AD 222-280)

According to the commentary, Wei Wendi, the emperor of the Wei Kingdom, asked one of his administrators about the art of strengthening his empire. The administrator then gave the following answer, "May you restore and esteem virtue. Carefully attend simple and basic matters diligently day and night, that's all." From that time on, Wei Wendi carefully practiced what the administrator had advised.

Therefore, the commentator used this proverb to describe the actions of Wei Wendi. How diligently he kept sharpening himself like sharpening a knife. As the emperor of the Wei empire, he did not deviate after he acquired the advice. Based on the proverb, the emperor worked very hard with self-discipline.

This proverb originated in ancient times; however, twenty-first century leaders can use its wisdom today. If you want to become a respected leader, you should learn how to sharpen yourself like sharpening a knife.

Chinese proverb: xin guan shang ren san ba huo.

新官上任三把火。

Translation: A new leader carries three torches of fire.

Meaning: New officers may apply strict measures.

Application: "A new leader carries three torches of fire" depicts the state of mind of a newly appointed leader. In general, a new leader will attempt to make improvements in operations by implementing changes. The three torches of fire refer to the ambition of the new leader. In other words, the new leader arrives with a definite drive.

What should we expect with leadership changes? Let's analyze this from two different perspectives. First, from the mindset of the new leader, and secondly from the perspective of the subordinates.

The new leader wants to make a good impression and perform very well. He or she has several reasons for doing this. First, the leader wants to please his/her own boss. Secondly, the new leader wants to implement methods and skills which he/she learned in leadership training. The new leader may want to make changes to rules and methods which his/her predecessors had implemented. The existing regulations may become obsolete and new rules will be announced and enforced. All of these changes will result from the strong ambition of the newly appointed leader.

Subordinates will have a much different perspective of leadership changes. They have become comfortable and good at working with the current system. When they first learn that leadership will be changing, they should begin to prepare to make changes. A positive step which subordinates should take is to establish in their mind that they will start a harmonious relationship with their new leader. The subordinates should completely cooperate and support the new leader. This is the right thing to do. It will not only make themselves look good but will also make their new leader look good.

If a subordinate feels that he/she definitely will not be able to work with the new leader, this person may need to transfer to a new position or to a new job. Trying to work against a new leader who carries three torches of fire is not the right thing to do.

Chinese proverb: yan bi you zhong.

言必有中。

Translation: Whenever one speaks, one speaks to the point.

Meaning: One speaks very precisely.

Application: Effective speakers are very precise with their words. These speakers will choose words carefully and create statements which are descriptive, accurate and to the point. Excess words will be avoided as distracting and time wasting. Speakers who convey their thoughts and minds with very precise speeches, they will capture the attention of their audience.

When I was growing up, there was a man in my neighborhood who rarely communicated with the neighbors. When this man did speak, however, everyone listened. All the neighbors knew that if this person wanted to communicate with them, it must be a very important message.

Leaders would do well to remember and follow this proverb. When they make speeches, they should be clear, precise and to the point. Speaking to the point is both an art and a skill which can be learned. It takes practice and work to become an interesting and precise orator. Leaders who know the art of speech can express their thoughts precisely without wasting any words, they will always attract the attention of their audience. A person who speaks to the point is like a hammer that hits the nail on the head.

Chinese proverb: yi ma dang xian.

一马当先。

Translation: One horse is ahead of other horses.

Meaning: It is the leading horse.

Application: If one horse is ahead of other horses, then this horse must be the leading horse. Of course, This proverb is a metaphor. As metaphor, it implies that human beings, like horses, need leaders. An individual can become a leader if this individual is able to demonstrate his or her leadership capability. According to the proverb, a leader must be ahead of other individuals. By doing so, the leader then can provide a path for the followers. If leaders really understand the principle of being the leading "horse", then they certainly will have followers.

Chinese proverb: zhi ji zhi bi, bai zhan bai sheng.

知己知彼，百战百胜。

Translation: If you know yourself and your opponents, you can win a hundred battles.

Meaning: Know both sides to obtain success.

Application: The teaching of "Know both sides to obtain success" is profound, and it has two applications. The first application is regarding militaries; and the second application is for ordinary citizens.

From a military perspective, if a leader wants to win a battle, he must learn as much as he can about his enemy and fully understand his own strengths and weaknesses. Prior to engaging in warfare, military leaders must know the tactics, armaments, combat strength, and morale of their opponents. With this knowledge in hand, they can develop detailed plans to fight and win battles. If military leaders can indeed discern themselves and their opponents, they can triumph a hundred times during a hundred combats.

As ordinary people, we don't face the enemy on a battlefield. We civilians typically work at various corporations where we have our own kinds of battles. The battles, which we face every day, may be labor law issues, productivity issues, marketing issues and others. All of these issues need to be solved by the management teams. For this reason, managers should always remember what this proverb teaches. When we really know ourselves and our opponents, we can create winning strategies. The winning concept in this proverb is really quite simple. Leaders must know both themselves and their opponents to win. To know ourselves, we need to identify our strengths and limitations. We must also know the strengths and limitations of the other side. The strategy of this proverb can enable us to go into a hundred conflicts with a hundred successes.

CHAPTER 6

Longevity

Chinese proverb: chang ming bai sui.

长命百岁。

Translation: Live a long life to one hundred years of age.

Meaning: To hope for a long life.

Application: Most people would like to live a long life on earth; you may agree that it is the normal desire of humankind. This Chinese proverb can accurately express the human desire of prolonged existence. The first two characters, 长命, indicate a long life, and the characters, 百岁, specify exactly one hundred years of age. You can understand how this proverb conveys your fellow living being's cheerful hope.

You can expect to see Chinese people display this kind of cheerfulness on two occasions. One of them would be at a new birth. Chinese people usually apply auspicious words to give their blessings to a newly born baby. The other occasion would be at elderly people's birthday gatherings. The wish of a long life for elderly people may give them an optimistic hope.

Chinese proverb: chang sheng bu lao.

长生不老。

Translation: People may live a long life and never get old.

Meaning: Live forever.

Application: Chinese people originally used this proverb to point out the hopeful philosophy of humankind that we can live forever. It is true that everyone in this world wants to live forever. Today Chinese people apply this optimistic philosophy by using it as a blessing to everyone, and particularly to elderly people. Aging is a reality, and this reality is applicable to all human beings. While people are still young, they may not think about aging. When people begin to get older and consider the brevity of life, they definitely will face the issue of getting old. Every living being grows old. The "live forever" thought and hope expressed by this proverb sounds very cheery.

Chinese proverb: fan hou zou yi zou, huo dao jiu shi.

饭后走一走，活到九十九。

Translation: Stroll after each meal, one may live up to ninety-nine.

Meaning: One can get benefit by walking.

Application: "Stroll after each meal, one may live up to ninety-nine" provides a very practical health tip to all people who are able to walk. Walking is a very easy exercise, and exercise is one of the important components for living well. Therefore, every person young or old can benefit by strolling after each meal.

According to some health-related statistics, take a walk can indeed improve people's health. This data provides people another reason for strolling after each meal. In fact, you might want to make strolling after each meal a part of your daily health habit. This strolling can get you out into a natural environment and might allow you to speak a word of greeting to your neighbors.

Years ago, one of the great Chinese scholars revealed his longevity secrets to a television interviewer. When the interviewer asked the scholar about his secrets for a long life, the scholar gave the following reply, "I do not smoke, and I try to eat well. The third secret is that I stroll for about fifteen minutes after each meal." This scholar's own words echoed the truth of our current proverb.

Those of us who desire to live a very healthy and long life should follow the example of the scholar. They should not smoke, they should eat well, and they should take a stroll after each meal.

Chinese proverb: fan lao huan tong.

返老还童。

Translation: Return from old to youth.

Meaning: Relive one's life again.

Application: How marvelous could it be to relive one's life again? How can any mature human being go back to live as a child again? Is it possible? The answer may be no, however, having this dream in your heart may enable you to be young. As for this proverb, it originally comes from Daoism. The followers of the Dao believe that they can become celestial beings if they truly practice the way of the Dao.

Although Daoism is still in practice today, Chinese people now use this proverb to express kind wishes to elderly people. They hope that their kind blessing will allow the elderly people maintain youthful and vigorous attitude. Returning to youth from old age might not be possible, however, as long as your heart is young, you may never truly be old.

Chinese proverb: fu shou shuang quan.

福寿双全。

Translation: Have both happiness and longevity.

Meaning: People may live an incredibly prosperous life.

Application: In China, those who have lived a prosperous and long life are considered to be incredibly blessed human beings. Most people in this world do not live incredibly wonderful lives. Many individuals have personally told me that life is very hard for them. The number of people in this world who actually live a long and wonderful life may be very small. For this reason, they certainly deserve compliments and admiration.

This proverb is used to convey admiration and praise to family members and friends who have the great fortune of living a happy and very long life.

CHAPTER 7

Opportunity

Chinese proverb: biao xin li yi.

标新立异。

Translation: Make something new and different.

Meaning: Create your own style.

Application: We now begin a new chapter, and it is focused on opportunities. I believe that people, throughout the whole world, are thrilled about new opportunities. It is because all of us want to live an exciting life.

This proverb talks about the concept of making something new and different. If you are an innovative individual, you may create many marvelous opportunities for yourself. These new opportunities could be anything within a wide range, from a new business to new hobbies. The new things which you create and try out will not just be beneficial to you, but also they can provide other people with refreshing feelings and thoughts.

My mother once gave me advice regarding fashion styles. She told me that she had started creating styles of her own when she was young. My mother did not follow the conventions of the day. For example, when the fashion of the day was to wear the color brown, my mother would wear something other than brown. She wanted to create something new and different. My mother thought that if most people follow the same fashion trend, it could be dull. I believe that my mother had a very good point. Individuals should be distinctive and always on the lookout to "Make something new and different".

Chinese proverb: bie kai sheng mian.

别开生面。

Translation: Humankind needs to break a new path.

Meaning: People can generate brand-new things.

Application: This proverb is similar to the previous proverb. The previous proverb is regarding making something new and different. Here, it addresses the idea of breaking a new path. To break a new path involves generating something that has never set its foot in the world before. Many individuals have become renowned by breaking a new path. We can use Albert Einstein as one example.

Albert Einstein was one of the universally renowned individuals. In 1905, he introduced his special theory of relativity. In addition to that, ten years later, Einstein introduced his general theory of relativity. He, at that point, became a very distinguished physicist. Albert Einstein opened up a brand-new path in physics. In 1921, Einstein received the Nobel Prize in Physics because of his creative thinking, hard work, intelligence, and strength.

Chinese proverb: cang qi dai shi.

藏器待时。

Translation: Hide the instrument until the time comes.

Meaning: Wait for the opportunity and then demonstrate your skill.

Application: This proverb teaches a strategy for your skills. The "instrument" stated above implies a skill which you have, and the recommendation is to hide the skill until the appropriate time arrives to demonstrate the skill. You may ask, "How long do I need to hide my skill?" This cannot be known in advance. It all depends when the correct opportunity arrives. Besides, patience is one of the great virtues for humankind, and you must be patient. As long as you have the skill, your time will come. While you are patiently waiting for your opportunity, you can improve your existing skill and accumulate more skills. When the moment of your opportunity arrives, you must not hesitate to reveal your abilities. In other words, you will let your talents be known at the exact right time.

One of my classmates in middle school has a brother who had good looks and talent. He wanted to become an actor. After he graduated from high school, the only opportunity he had was to be a farmer. While he was tilling the field, he kept practicing his mandarin speaking skill, because he knew that his mandarin must be perfect to be an actor. He waited patiently for his opportunity. It took several years until one day his opportunity suddenly came. He took that chance and went for a stage test. Everything went very well, and he eventually became a stage actor.

Chinese proverb: chen re da tie.

趁热打铁。

Translation: Strike while the iron is hot.

Meaning: Take the opportunity at the right moment.

Application: Strike is an action. When a piece of iron is hot, a black smith will strike it to fashion it into something he wants. This proverb instructs us to taking opportunities at an appropriate time. As a parable, this proverb uses heat and iron to teach us a good concept. We may consider ourselves to be black smiths and think like a black smith.

As a black smith, you must strike the iron when you see that it is truly hot. Due to the hot heat, you can fashion the iron to the shape you need. The "heat" represents the condition, and to "strike" indicates to take the opportunity. Therefore, when the condition is "hot", it is the precise moment to take the opportunity. When the moment has just arrived, you absolutely must take action.

Chinese proverb: da you ke wei.

大有可为。

Translation: There are big opportunities in the world.

Meaning: A bright future is ahead.

Application: According to this Chinese proverb, there are big opportunities in the world for every person. In other words, everyone can have a bright future. If you can visualize a bright future, you will have it. Better yet, a bright future does not even have an age limit. You possibly heard of the story about the founder of Kentucky Fried Chicken, Colonel Harland Sanders. His story is very encouraging to people around the world who would like to seek big opportunities.

Colonel Harland Sanders enjoyed cooking when he was just a young man. He was particularly good at cooking fried chicken. He eventually turned his cooking skills into a business. Colonel Harland Sanders started his fried chicken franchise at the age when most people would be retired. The business which Colonel Sanders started was a great success and he sold it at a great profit.

The story of Colonel Sanders can be a great inspiration to you. He used skills which he already possessed to grab for a big opportunity. You can say that his bright future began at a late age.

Doing business has no age limit, whether you are young or old. It is up to you whether you seek your opportunity or not. If you seek hard and thoroughly enough, a bright future could be indeed right ahead.

Chinese proverb: shi bu yi chi.

事不宜迟。

Translation: Lose no time to attend the matter.

Meaning: Take care of certain matters immediately.

Application: According to this proverb, certain things in this world have a time limit. When a certain important matter is very urgent, we need to take care of it immediately.

If your plumbing should start leaking, and water is pouring into your home; or the brakes on your car are failing, it is time to act. Saving a life can be an urgent matter with a short time limit. When you happen to come across someone who needs help desperately, you must lose no time at all to offer a helping hand. If you pass an opportunity to help someone in a desperate situation, then someday your conscience will weigh heavily on you.

Chinese proverb: shi tong yun tai.

时通运泰。

Translation: Attain prosperity at the right time.

Meaning: When prosperity arrives, everything goes well.

Application: Have you ever experienced the attaining prosperity referred to by this proverb? I humbly believe that you have either experienced it or you will have the opportunity to experience it in the future. You may ask if this is true. The answer is yes. This proverb states a reality. Life does have delightful and prosperous periods for every human being. These blessings can be financial, or they might be a dream come true. The prosperity may arrive unexpectedly, however, it will arrive just when you need it. You could experience one or more of the things in the following list:

- You become a wealthy heir.

- You find your ideal match at the perfect time.

- You get your desired promotion.

- You have extremely intelligent offspring.

- You obtained your dream occupation.

- You profit from your investment in abundance.

The list can go on; however, you get the point. Everything will go very well for you when prosperity opens up its big doors for you at the ideal time. If you are still waiting for opportunity to come, then you must be patient. No matter what, you need to tell yourself without hesitation that "Attain prosperity at the right time" is a reality.

Chinese proverb: ying ji li duan.

应机立断。

Translation: Make a quick decision when opportunity suddenly comes.

Meaning: Do not hesitate to respond to chance.

Application: This proverb suggests that when a sudden opportunity arrives, people should respond very quickly. In other words, if an unexpected opportunity comes to you, you must not hesitate to make a decision. Otherwise, the opportunity could disappear right away.

Decision-making is very normal. We make decisions every day. Some decisions are very important, and other decisions can be quite trivial. Whatever the consequences of the matter are, we must be decisive. It is very important that we need to trust our own judgement.

What are the opportunities which this proverb references? They could be anything. You might meet the potential love of your life. You might have randomly met a potential investor for your new business. When these opportunities arrive, you must make a positive decision.

I remember a nine years old girl who lived next door to my best friend. This young girl had always wanted to become a principal dancer. Her parents had obliged her wishes and sent her to a dancing school. One day, the representatives from the Beijing dancing school had arrived in Shanghai and were looking for talent. The parents of this young girl heard this news and acted quickly. They brought her to the auditions. Everything worked out wonderfully and the girl was accepted into the school. Even though she had to leave her family to study in Beijing, the family decided without any hesitation that it was the chance for her to fulfill her dream.

CHAPTER 8

Relationships

Chinese proverb: ai bu shi shou.

爱不释手。

Translation: One lovingly holds tight a favorable treasure.

Meaning: Treasure someone extremely.

Application: Human relationships are very important to all of us. On the first page of this chapter, we will place emphasis on the human love relationship. This proverb comes from the Qing dynasty (AD 1644-1911). During that period, people used this proverb to describe a person who loved something or someone extremely. When a person enjoyed one particular object, this person would not leave without the treasure; and when someone fell in love, the person would treasure the person he/she loved.

We can agree that genuine love can knit people together for life. When one person truly loves another person and that love is mutual, then the two people may never leave each other as long as they both live. True love relationships have always existed in history, and of course they still exist today. Either we ourselves have experienced such genuine love, or we have witnessed this proverb described above. The following true story can validate the point of this proverb.

Once upon a time, a very ordinary gentleman lived in China. Although he was very nice, he was a rather poor man. His father passed away very early in his life, and he was the only child in the family. He did not plan to get married, because he wanted to take very good care of his mother.

One day, the company he worked for appointed him as a mentor to a new employee, and this new employee happened to be a lovely girl. He taught his pupil what he knew in a professional way. In like manner, the pupil respected her mentor as well. Months passed, and the lovely girl fell in love with her mentor. The pupil treasured her mentor extremely and vice versa; the mentor loved his pupil as if she were the only treasure he ever held in his life. Then all of a sudden, a disapproval human storm lashed out. Almost everyone who knew both the mentor and the apprentice was against the pure love relationship. They ridiculed both of them. The atmosphere was extremely difficult all because of the age gap between the two.

The mentor was almost as old as the girl's parents. Even though the two of them faced tremendous challenges, they were truly in love, and they treasured each other tremendously. The love between the two was so strong that no one could break it. Eventually they became husband and wife.

This story tells us a truth. When two people are really in deep love, they cannot live without each other. Moreover, this story can also declare a truth to the whole world that if love is indeed genuine, then nothing can destroy it. Humankind may destroy most everything; however, they can never destroy true love. True love is absolutely the strongest thing on earth!

Chinese proverb: ai wu ji wu.

爱屋及乌。

Translation: One's love for a house extends even to a crow on one's roof.

Meaning: Love everything your mate loves.

Application: This proverb uses a parable to describe a love relationship. Suppose you are deeply in love, then the "house" mentioned above actually implies a person whom you are in love with. The "crow" indicates whatever your lover adores. When you are truly in love with someone, you will not just love that person but also love whatever that person adores, even it is a crow. The crow designates something that is not lovable. When you are in love, however, if your lover adores a crow, you will like the crow as well.

The point of this proverb is this: An authentic love relationship will testify everything. If your mate raises rabbits, for example, you will also learn to care for rabbits. Even though you normally do not like any type of small animals, because of your true love for your mate, you will begin to appreciate the rabbits. When you love a person sincerely, you will enjoy whatever your lover enjoys.

Chinese proverb: ba dao xiang zhu.

拔刀相助。

Translation: One pulls out a knife to help.

Meaning: A person assists without reservation.

Application: "One pulls out a knife to help" is a statement, and this statement indicates that someone wants to help others wholeheartedly. The statement "pulls out a knife" may sound drastic, it is used to suggest that a person is willing to assist other people without the slightest reservation.

According to Chinese tradition, if one person really wants to help another person, then the helper must do their very best. When you see your friend or someone experiencing difficulty or danger, you will provide the assistance all you can without any hesitation. If you look for ways to apply this principle of helping people, you will be ready to act when the need arises.

Chinese proverb: ba mian ling long.

八面玲珑。

Translation: One deals in eight different facets smoothly.

Meaning: One applies the art of diplomacy.

Application: Human relationships are extremely complex. If someone asks you why people in this world do not agree on everything, you can come up with a variety of answers. The complex nature of human relationships requires great skill to reach agreements between different individuals and groups. This is what is meant by having to deal in eight different facets smoothly. When skill and wisdom are used with the art of diplomacy, differences between people of different backgrounds, cultures, languages, and personalities can be smoothed and resolved.

Chinese proverb: bai tou xie lao.

白头偕老。

Translation: Stay together all the way to old age.

Meaning: Live as a devoted couple to the end.

Application: "Stay together all the way to old age" primarily describes the relationship between a husband and a wife. The first two characters of this proverb, 白头, specify "white haired head", and then the last two characters, 偕老, indicate "year after year to stay with each other to the very end." Hence, this proverb portrays husband and wife as a devoted couple. For people to remain in a good marriage, both husband and wife must treat each other with genuine love, respect, and kindness. If they do, they can get along very well. As the result of love, respect, and kindness, they will certainly live as a devoted couple to the end.

Chinese proverb: bei dao er chi.

背道而驰。

Translation: One runs in the opposite direction.

Meaning: A person is rebellious.

Application: This proverb can be used to describe the actions of a rebellious child in a parent-child relationship. Parents desire obedient children, and children however often behave contrary to the advice given by their parents. Why do they repeatedly conduct themselves like that? The answer could be one or more of the items listed below:

1. They are simply rebellious.

2. They want their parents to bear some pain.

3. They consider themselves smarter than their parents.

Regardless of what caused the children to run in the opposite direction, it will hurt the parents without any doubt. Then what can parents do to prevent their children from disrespectful behavior? The following paragraphs provide some ideas for parents whose children often show rebellious conduct.

Parents should first set a good example for their children. They need to teach their children right from wrong and they need to do right things so that their children will learn from them. It is very important that parents establish family rules so that the children will know what is expected of them.

Sometimes, children need to learn from their own mistakes. Even when parents set a good example, establish family rules, and provide sound advice, children may do the opposite of what is right. Although this is difficult to go through, very often rebellious children will begin to taste the negative results of their behavior and return to doing right. Lessons learned in reality may be much better than those given by their parents.

Children who consider themselves smarter than their parents have inflated egos. As time goes by, they will learn that they are wrong. As children grow and become intellectually mature enough, many of the earlier disobedient behaviors will disappear. Then the children will begin to appreciate the wisdom that their parents had all along.

Chinese proverb: bei xin qi yi.

背信弃义。

Translation: One betrays.

Meaning: It is a breach of faith.

Application: There exists one type of human being in this world who is disloyal. A disloyal individual should not be trusted. I recommend two actions in dealing with disloyalty. The first action is that we ourselves must never fall into that category. The second action is that we should watch out for and avoid those who are perfidious in our friendship circle.

One of my nieces experienced an incident that absolutely shocked her. She once completely trusted a class-mate from her high school and considered that person to be her "best friend" forever. Both her friend and the friend's mother earned low income wages. My niece is exceptionally compassionate and generous. When the friend needed oral surgery and could not afford the operation, my niece paid the expenses of her friend's operation. Instead of being grateful for the help she received, the friend became jealous of my niece's good paying job. The "best friend" then made public knowledge personal secrets that my niece had entrusted only to her. When my niece discovered the disloyalty from her "best friend", she was totally shaken and sad.

I told my niece, for the benefit of both sides, to reassess the friendship. Unfaithful friends can bring more harm than they are worth. For our own good, I believe that disloyal friends do not belong in our friendship circle.

Chinese proverb: bi xue dan xin.

碧血丹心。

Translation: A person sheds blood with a loyal heart.

Meaning: One is truly faithful.

Application: In absolute contrast to the previous proverb, this proverb describes faithfulness. The proverb, 碧血丹心, came from a true event recorded in Chinese history. Based on the record, the event unfolds like this: An officer was extremely loyal to a high-ranking official. Enemies of the high-ranking official killed the officer out of hatred for his faithfulness. According to legend, three years after this faithful officer died, his blood turned into jasper stone.

What could this event reveal to people? It reveals to us that truly faithful people exist in the world. Even though the recorded event happened very long ago, truly faithful people still exist today. If you have will power and a sincere heart, you yourself can become a faithful person to those you really care about. These people include your family and friends. On the other hand, you may be looking for people with a heart that is loyal to you. Trustworthiness works both ways. When you are loyal to your family and friends, they may be loyal to you as well.

Chinese proverb: bi yi shuang fei.

比翼双飞。

Translation: Two birds fly side by side.

Meaning: Two people are dedicated to each other.

Application: This proverb uses the natural phenomenon of two lovebirds flying side by side to refer to the human love relationship. The type of bird referenced in the proverb is a very unique type. This type of bird will never be seen flying alone, he is always accompanied by his mate. Chinese people use this phenomenon to highlight the love of couples who are entirely dedicated to each other. Couples who are just as dedicated as the lovebirds always stay together.

Chinese proverb: bing dong san chi, fei yi ri zhi han.

冰冻三尺，非一日之寒。

Translation: Three feet deep of ice is not formed in one day.

Meaning: The trouble has been brewing for quite some time.

Application: Ice is one form of water. When the temperature reaches the freezing point, water will turn to ice. We know that it takes more than just one day to accumulate three feet deep of ice on the ground. This proverb uses the phenomenon of ice to depict the cold status of some human relationships. Three feet deep of frozen ice indicates that the trouble a particular relationship has been brewing for quite some time.

What can we do to prevent relationships from turning into cold ice? There are many things we can and should do. In general, we are often self-centered and not concerned enough about others. We often allow ourselves to react instead being proactive. Many issues might never arise or may be resolved by themselves if people would be proactive in showing concern for others. If you sense there is trouble developing in your relationships with family, friends, or fellow workers, you need to uncover the cause of the discontented feelings as soon as possible. Particularly for friendships you would like to keep. Once you discover the cause, you need to take active steps to resolve the problems. If you caused the problem unintentionally, you need to apologize first and then take necessary steps to warm up the relationship.

Typically, a good relationship takes two things to maintain. These two things are time and money. Yes, the two basic elements of maintaining good human friendships are time and money. If you think it over very carefully, you will admit what has been discussed here is correct. For that reason, you may want to spend time with others and spending money to enjoy life with others.

Chinese proverb: bing xiao wa jie.

冰消瓦解。

Translation: Ice is melted and tile is disintegrated.

Meaning: Issues are dissolvable.

Application: This proverb uses objects such as ice and tile to indicate that some objects are dissolvable. The proverb implies that people can make issues disappear. The "ice" and "tile" are metaphors for issues in life. Ice is a very cold object, and a tile is a very hard object. They both give the impression of being difficult to handle. Nevertheless, when the temperature rises above the freezing point, the solid cold ice can be melted. As for the tile, it is hard, yet brittle, and the tile is certainly breakable.

We know from physics; heat can melt ice and force can break tile. Therefore, both objects are dissolvable. Now we can apply this dissolvable concept to our human relationships. Every day we can face relationship issues. At a family level, we can have issues with our parents or siblings. From a personal level, we may have issues with our friends or co-workers.

Where do these issues come from? The issues come from the fact that people have different points of view. All of us are unique human beings. Our different points of view can originate from a multitude of diverse factors. These can include family, finance, job, life, school and politics, etc. With all of these differences, it is no wonder that we do not always see eye to eye.

Then should we become individuals who just agree with everyone on everything? No, we need to remain true to ourselves and hold our points of view. However, we need to soften our communications with others and let them maintain their own opinions. People will never agree on everything. The key point here is to dissolve issues.

If you place a piece of ice in a warm environment, the ice will be melted. Similarly, if you toss a piece of rigid tile out of your hands, the rigidness of tile will be gone. If you are starting to see the picture which this proverb paints clearly, then you understand that you should be the person who will make issues disappear. How can you do it? You must first melt your own icy heart and break your rigid spirit toward any existing problems or wounds. You will then have the pleasure of watching issues evaporate.

Chinese proverb: bu bei bu kang.

不卑不亢。

Translation: People should be neither subservient nor arrogant.

Meaning: One must behave with dignity.

Application: According to this proverb, relationships between individuals need to be authentic and poised. If you are too submissive, or you are too arrogant, you will be viewed as an artificial individual. The point here is that people need to behave themselves with dignity. All human beings are created equal. You should be yourself. This means that you need to behave naturally and gracefully. If you are too submissive, you appear inferior; if you are too arrogant, you appear superior. The best relationships occur when all parties in the relationship conduct themselves with dignity.

Chinese proverb: bu bian zhen wei.

不辨真伪。

Translation: One is unable to distinguish truth versus false.

Meaning: A person has no knowledge of deceitfulness.

Application: When an individual is unable to distinguish between truth and lies, then this individual will experience disappointments and suffering. It seems like common sense to assume that people should recognize what is truth from what is false. However, the reality not always present people with such a case.

Why do not all human beings in this world recognize truth from false? Well, it is because people are different. The differences include their beliefs, culture, and personality. For these reasons, some people may not be aware of deceitfulness, especially in people they trust.

The following true story provides an example of deceitfulness not being recognized: There was a couple who appeared to be in a good husband and wife relationship. Together, they raised a son and a daughter. The children lived a happy life with their parents. Years went by, and everything appeared peaceful in the family. Nevertheless, one day, the daughter discovered a big secret; and this secret absolutely shocked her! She discovered that her father actually had another family. She was very scared to tell her mother the discovery, so she kept it to herself. A few years later, the wife finally knew what was going on with her husband.

There are dishonest people in the world. These people may pretend to be honest; therefore, it can be very difficult to distinguish the truth from lies. The wife in the story had no knowledge of her husband's deceitfulness. It may be that she was so honest herself that she could never imagine someone she loved could do such terrible things. As we consider this proverb, there is a reality which we should keep in mind. The reality is that no one can cover the truth forever. The truth will eventually be revealed!

Chinese proverb: bu yi jiao.

布衣交。

Translation: Make friends with the poor.

Meaning: Become friends with the impoverished.

Application: My parents and grandparents were land owners prior to 1949. Land, social status and most material possessions were all lost before I was born. I have an older sister and a brother. As I was once very poor, I understand the feelings of poor and needy people.

I can relate to the proverb in my own personal life. While I was poor, I did have a few people who became dear friends to me, and I will always be very grateful for them. These people were much better off than I was, and yet they had never showed pride or haughtiness toward me. Therefore, these cherished individuals will always remain in my memory as long as I live.

I may never forget about one particular event occurred in my life. Although the event appeared insignificant, it absolutely had very significant impact on me. That event happened during the Chinese Cultural Revolution when I was about twelve years of age. I would like to share that small occurrence in the following paragraph.

One morning, I was standing at a street corner in Downtown Shanghai reading an article posted on the wall. While I was reading, a very kind voice came to my ears. I turned around and saw my former classmate's wealthy father smile at me. He asked me how I had been. His amiable smile and kind words touched my heart. We talked briefly, and then he went on his away. After he left, I said to myself that I should not be discouraged, because there were kind people in the world.

The former classmate's father could have just walked by without saying a word to me, yet, his kindness lit up my sorrowful heart. I never met this man again and yet I will remember his kindness all of my life.

During the same period of my youth, I had a friend from school named Rumei. Although Rumei came from a wealthy family and I came from a poor family, we were best friends. We spent many hours playing together. We went shopping together and I spent hours at her house. My house was small and not nice enough for parties; however, I was always welcome as a guest at Rumei's house whenever she and her brother had a gathering.

Making friends with the poor can prove to be a blessing to you, and you may be a blessing to your friends. Your friendship will give you an understanding of those who are not as fortunate as you are. You will often find that those who do not possess a great amount of wealth are more open, giving and interesting to talk to.

My father once asked me to consider the pawns on a chess board. The pawns are not rich or powerful, however, every pawn is important. My father told me that the loss of pawns could cause lead to the loss of the king. The point my father wanted to make was that poor people can sometimes be a great help to you.

Chinese proverb: chun chi xiang yi.

唇齿相依。

Translation: Lips and teeth depend on each other intimately.

Meaning: It is a very close relationship.

Application: All people in this world know that lips and teeth are very close to each other. They are mutually dependent on each other. The relationship between them is so close that one must stay with another. Without lips, teeth will not survive well; similarly, without teeth, lips would be extremely uncomfortable. Therefore, they really need each other.

This close relationship can be applied to your own family relationships. Indeed, your family members need each other just like the lips and the teeth need each other. Without each other's support, families may fall apart. When one member of the family encounters difficulties, other members need to show their love, care, and support. If these elements of support are not there, then the individual and also the family might be devastated. On the other hand, when all members of the family give their love, care, and support, then the difficulties of the family member in need are shared and overcome.

By supporting each other, every member receives benefit. Therefore, just as lips and teeth depend on each other, family members must also stay together and support one another.

Chinese proverb: chun wang chi han.

唇亡齿寒。

Translation: When lips perish, teeth are cold.

Meaning: Survive together or perish together.

Application: This proverb states the reality that lips and teeth must survive together, or else they will perish together. We can clearly see that this proverb is a metaphor. It implies that if two vitally related entities do not support each other, then both of these entities will not survive. The implication is that related entities must stay together to protect each other.

People may apply this proverb to relationships concerning their family, neighbors, community, and even the entire world. You can ask yourself a few questions. Should you take care of your own family members? The answer is yes. It does not matter which member you are; you unquestionably have a specific duty or role. Do you need your neighbors? You certainly do. If you establish a friendly relationship with your neighbors, you will have a sense of security. This notion can also extend to neighboring countries and even the whole world.

A wise person might meditate on the principle of this proverb and consider the multitude of implications and ramifications. This meditation may lead to actions which could strengthen families, neighbors, countries and the world.

Chinese proverb: da shi hua xiao, xiao shi hua liao.

大事化小, 小事化了。

Translation: People should resolve big issues into small issues and then into no issues.

Meaning: It is a problem-solving strategy.

Application: Every person may face either big or small problems every day. Many of these problems are relationship issues. Problems are like headaches, and people do not like them. Life is much more pleasant when problems are resolved.

Can people make issues disappear? Is it possible? According to this Chinese proverb, it is very possible. This proverb is like a magic wand; it teaches people to make issues disappear. The secret here is to turn large issues into small issues and resolve these small issues. Once this is done, the problem will vanish.

This approach can be used to solve any problem. With relationship problems, it involves establishing a common ground between individuals. After the common ground is established, then negotiations on small issues take place to come up with an agreeable solution. The following true story illustrates one of the methods that people often use to resolve issues.

One night after teaching a class, a college instructor walked out of the school building toward his car. A young man followed him. The instructor noticed that someone was behind him and then he politely asked the young man if he needed help. The young man replied, "Yes, I need help." He then asked the young man what kind of help he wanted, and the young man replied, "a better grade."

The instructor realized that the young man was one of his students from the class which he had just dismissed. Then he quickly came up with an idea. He wanted the issue to be solved and decided to use negotiation as a tool. The instructor asked the student what grade he thought he deserved. The student hesitated for a brief moment. Then the teacher initiated a brief discussion regarding the students work. After their brief discussion, the young man stated that he believed a "B" should be good. This grade seemed reasonable to the teacher. At that moment, both the teacher and the student reached an agreement. That night, both of them went home with a peacefully heart.

Chinese proverb: feng yu tong zhou.

风雨同舟。

Translation: You and your friends are in the same storm-tossed boat.

Meaning: True friendship is being tested.

Application: No one wants to be in a storm-tossed boat. When the sailing is smooth, many "friends" will be happy to sail with you. When a terrible storm arises, most of these so-called friends will jump ship. If you are fortunate, you may have one or two real friends who are willing to weather the storm with you.

This proverb points to genuine friendships. When everything is going smoothly in your life, you often will be surrounded by many friends. In life, however, we encounter trials and predicaments. When overwhelming trials and troubles come upon you, you will find that almost all of your friends are one by one gone. As a result, the tough times you experience can allow you to distinguish between genuine friends and false friends.

We have a reason to be grateful for trials and troubles. They allow us to identify our faithful friends. These are the friends which will never desert us. We should always remember to remain true to our friends when they experience tough times in life. Genuine friends should stand together through thick and thin.

Chinese proverb: guang ming lei luo.

光明磊落。

Translation: Treat everyone honestly and aboveboard.

Meaning: Demonstrate genuine moral character.

Application: In this world, there exists a Golden Rule. Simply stated, the Golden Rule is "Do unto others as you would have them do unto you". The Golden Rule is a universal standard and measurement for the evaluation of conduct. Honest human beings will try to do their best to abide by this Golden Rule. Many people act like the Golden Rule does not exist.

This proverb encourages all of us to treat others honestly and aboveboard. We cannot control what others may do; however, we have a duty to demonstrate a genuine positive moral character. When you are honest and kind with people, others are much more likely to respond with kindness to you.

Chinese proverb: hai ren zhi xin bu ke you, fang ren zhi xin bu ke wu.

害人之心不可有，防人之心不可无。

Translation: Never have a heart to harm others; always have a heart to protect self.

Meaning: One must never hurt others; one should always shield self.

Application: This proverb teaches people two very important principles in human relationships. These two principles contain so much wisdom that by following them life becomes more peaceful and enjoyable. Let's examine these two principles.

The first principle is one of prevention. It warns and tries to prevent us from doing wrong to others. We must never have a heart to harm others. It is an evil heart that would like to deliberately harm and destroy another human being. To harm people is a crime and we must never do that!

The second principle is one of protection. It states that you should always have a vigilant heart to protect yourself. You need to be careful and avoid being hurt. If you safeguard yourself with a vigilant heart, you and your family will perhaps avoid much regret. Remember that every human being needs to be responsible for both: never harm others; always protect self.

Chinese proverb: he qi zhi xiang.

和气致祥。

Translation: Politeness may obtain good fortune.

Meaning: Kindness can have benefit.

Application: According to this proverb, if you are constantly gentle and kind to others, you might very possibly receive good fortune someday. Can this be true? You perhaps have some reservations about believing this saying. My hope is that after you read the following commentary and meditate on the proverb, you will definitely believe it to be true.

Suppose there are two individuals asking you for a favor. The first person asks for the favor using a very demanding language; the second person asks you with a very polite tone. To whom will you be more likely to grant the favor? The answer would be to the second person. Human beings usually prefer the nice and gracious approach.

When people treat you with kindness and compassion, your heart will feel very pleasant. When people use their complaining and demanding manner, you probably would have very negative thoughts about them. You may want to bless those who have always been kind to you. Vice versa, if you treat others with a sincere heart all the time, you might receive blessings from them. The story below provides an illustration of this proverb from real life.

Once there was a postal worker who delivered mail in a certain area. An elderly woman was one of the customers on his route. The postal worker had always been kind to this woman. Every time the postal worker gave the women her mail, he would say hello with a gentle smile.

Then one day the woman made a small request of the postal worker. She asked, "Would you please come to see me for a few minutes on your day off?" The postal worker responded "yes". From that time on, the elderly woman had a visitor every Sunday for a few minutes chat. Years passed, the woman got older. Then one day the postal worker received a notification. The letter informed him to attend a meeting at a lawyer's office. When all of the attendees gathered at the lawyer's office, the lawyer read the woman's will. The woman left $100,000 to the postal worker for his kindness.

The postal worker perhaps never thought of any reward. However, he was compassionate enough to take a few minutes out of his day off to be kind. The prize he received was due to his consistent good deeds. His weekly visitation for a few minutes chat with the elderly woman was a great kindness that he bestowed upon that lonely soul.

Based on this proverb, politeness may obtain a good fortune. Therefore, the postal worker received his reward by being kind on a regular basis. This story is just one example of a multitude of similar acts of kindness which take place in the world.

Chinese proverb: jin zhu zhe chi, jin mo zhe hei.

近朱者赤, 近墨者黑。

Translation: Near red ink, you will get a red stain; near black ink, you will get a black stain.

Meaning: You will be influenced by your close friends.

Application: You may have heard the saying "You are what you eat." It might be true that if you eat healthy foods regularly, you perhaps will be healthy. On the other hand, if you frequently eat an unhealthy diet, you may not be healthy. Now let us apply a slight variation of this concept using color instead of food. If you are continually near red ink, you will get a red stain; if you are always near black ink, then you will get a black stain. The color here represents your close friends.

This proverb uses the parable of color to teach us a reality— that we need to be careful when we select close friends. Our close friends have a strong influence on us. Therefore, it is vitally important what kind of friends we associate with.

If your close friends work hard, you may try to work hard as well. Otherwise, you may not want to associate with them or they do not want you as a friend. If you have careless friends, you could also become just like them. Examine yourself right now; what color stain do you have?

Chinese proverb: liang bai ju shang.

两败俱伤。

Translation: Both sides are injured.

Meaning: No one wins.

Application: This proverb states a fact. The fact is that if two sides are engaged in a fight or a battle whether it is physical or psychological, damage is inevitable—both sides will be injured. If the injury is not physical damage, it will certainly cause an emotional wound. The result of fighting is injury, whether you appear to be on the winning side or on the losing side. In fights between relatives or personal friends, there will absolutely be no real winner. Instead of exchanging blows because of conflicting views, the differences need to be resolved with reasonable settlements.

Chinese proverb: liang mian san dao.

两面三刀。

Translation: One knife has two sides with three edges.

Meaning: It is very dangerous.

Application: Normal knives have two sides with only one edge. Where do the two sides with three edges come from? It is a metaphor to describe dangerous individuals. This proverb addresses a certain dangerous reality regarding some people.

The reality is that a type of people exists which you can never trust. A person who is like a knife that has two sides with three edges is tremendously dangerous. The danger from this type of person could be physical danger, emotional danger or both. If you know someone who fits in the description of this proverb, then you must be alert and careful. If you are an honest individual, then this proverb gives a warning that you must watch out!

In this world, there are people who almost all the time deal with others in a deceitfully manner and you need to be extremely cautious. The Chinese Cultural Revolution lasted for ten years. During part of this period, I was in junior high. A student transferred into our class. This girl was very friendly and wanted to be my friend. I confided the details of my family to her. My family had been relatively wealthy before 1949 and lost everything. Due to our past, we were persecuted during the Cultural Revolution. This person turned out to not be a friend, rather, she was a knife with two sides and three edges. She told my family information to others and added lies to make our family look terrible.

Let us use a coin as one example. A coin has two sides: one side represents you and the other side represents another person. On your side, you must never be treacherous. However, you should pay attention to the other side. If the other side is the untrustworthy type, you must think cautiously and deal with that individual very carefully and resourcefully.

Chinese proverb: liang quan qi mei.

两全其美。

Translation: Both sides should be content.

Meaning: Satisfy both parties.

Application: This proverb teaches a mutually beneficial principle. It indicates that when two entities are in a relationship, both entities should obtain satisfaction. The entities can be one of a wide variety of types.

The entity may differ; however, the concept is the same. Different types of entities include a nation-to-nation, family-to-family, or human-to-human relationship. Regardless of the entity type, the point is that both sides should be content. If you desire your relationship to last, then you need to apply the principle of "Both sides should be content". When both sides are truly satisfied, then two entities will have the genuine peace and contentment with each other.

Chinese proverb: jiang shan yi gai, ben xing nan yi.

江山易改, 本性难移。

Translation: It is easier to change rivers and mountains than change a person's nature.

Meaning: You can never change people.

Application: If you get to know your relatives and friends really well, you will tend to find their faults. After your discovery of other people's faults, you may even end up of trying to change them. It is particularly true of those you are very fond of; you want them to be like you. When people see your real nature, they either dislike you, or try to change you as well.

This proverb precisely points out a simple reality that it is easier to change rivers and mountains than to change a person's nature. In other words, you can never change anyone, and no one can change you either. You should never have the slightest intention to change anybody. You need to accept who they are and what they are. The very truth is that the only person, in this enormous world, you can change is yourself.

Chinese proverb: lu yao zhi ma li, ri jiu jian ren xin.

路遥知马力, 日久见人心。

Translation: As a long journey evaluates a horse's strength, time tells a person's heart.

Meaning: Time eventually reveals the true character of a person.

Application: This proverb teaches a valuable lesson regarding discernment. Distance and time are used to evaluate strength and character, respectively. As distance can be used to assess the strength of a horse, similarly, time will reveal the true heart of a person.

In our lifetime, we will meet numerous people. Most of them will only be acquaintances, and some of them will become our friends. We usually say, "How are you" and "Goodbye" to our acquaintances. We may share some of our deep thoughts to friends. Yet we must ask ourselves questions like, "How much can I share with my friends?" "How many of them are truly loyal to me?" Can we find out the true heart and loyalty our friends?

According to this proverb, we can find out for sure. The genuine heart of a human being will be revealed through time. As a long journey will reveal the strength of a horse, similarly, a long period of time will show true friendship. Will a friend stay loyal for a short time when things are going well? This is very likely. Will a friend remain true over years and years of good times? This will often occur. Will that friend remain true as you go through years of trials and sickness? This is very difficult for a friend to do, however, if you have a friend who has done this, then you have been fortunate and have found a loyal and true friend.

Chinese proverb: po jing chong yuan.

破镜重圆。

Translation: A broken mirror is united as one again.

Meaning: A separated couple is reunited.

Application: This proverb is based on a story. The true story is one of many interesting stories recorded in a book called 本事诗·情感 (The Collection of Stories in Verses by Meng Qi). This particular story, contained in the following paragraphs, is about a loving couple and their suffering. Even though the story was quite sad, the ending gives a sense of joy. Moreover, the story is very touching and fascinating. Now let the story begin.

The Chen Empire (AD 557-589) of the Southern dynasties became very frail, and it was about to perish. The empire however wanted to fight the last battle. It looked hopeless to win; therefore, the emperor's son-in-law predicted that he might be separated from his wife in that final battle. Therefore, he broke a brass mirror in half. He then gave half of the mirror to the princess, and he kept the other half. The son-in-law stated that if he and his wife reunited again, both of their half mirrors would be the proof. They even set a date to reunite, and that date was to be the fifteenth day of the first month in the following year. On that day, they each would need to offer to sell their half mirrors in the market of the capital in hopes of reuniting.

Sure enough, the son-in-law's prediction was correct. On the last battle, the Chen army was completely defeated, the Chen empire therefore vanished from history. Indeed, the battle separated the loving couple. In addition to that, the citizens of the former Chen empire were scattered and homeless.

The Chen empire's disappearance changed the status of its former nobles. The princess suddenly became a commoner overnight. Worse yet, the former princess became one of many captives to the conquerors.

As a captive, she lost her freedom, and had to serve as a maidservant to her master. Although she was not free, the maidservant was fortunate to have a place to stay.

On the fifteenth of the first month in the following year, the husband of the former princess kept his promise, and he went to the market of the capital city to sell his half mirror. He even wrote a poem on the mirror: "The mirror and the person were both lost. The mirror is here, but the person is not. There is no shadow of Chang e; only the empty light of the moon is here."

The son-in-law was consistently and persistently trying to sell his precious possession in the market; however, not a single person was interested in buying it. In reality, as he called out offering his mirror for sale, his heart was listening and longing to hear the voice of another seller of a half mirror. The odd merchandise for sale eventually caught people's attention, and they found out the real motive of the man selling the half mirror.

The news spread. It reached the ears of Yang Su, master of the former princess. After master Yang Su learned the story of the couple and their half mirrors, he allowed the husband to meet his wife. The master then gave the princess her freedom and the couple was reunited. The broken mirror was united as one again.

This touching story tells that if two people are truly in deep love, nothing in the whole world can separate them. No matter what happened or what will happen, true love will eventually prevail.

Note: In a fairy tale, Chang e is the goddess of the moon.

Chinese proverb: ren yi zou, cha jiu liang.

人一走，茶就凉。

Translation: After the person is gone, the tea is cold.

Meaning: People need to maintain their friendships.

Application: Drinking hot tea is a wonderful Chinese tradition enjoyed by millions. There are many varieties of tea and everyone seems to have a favorite. When a cup of tea is freshly brewed and poured into your cup, the fresh aroma fills the air. The taste of the tea is pleasing. Once your tea begins to cool, you will want to add more hot tea into your cup. When a cup of hot tea gets cold, the tea is not pleasant to drink.

"After the person is gone, the tea is cold" implies that we need to constantly maintain and nurture personal relationships. This requires time, effort and respect for others. If we do not maintain our relationships, they will end up like a cup of tea that has gone cold. In other words, the relationship ends.

Chinese proverb: tu zi bu chi wo bian cao.

兔子不吃窝边草。

Translation: A rabbit does not eat the grass around its own hole.

Meaning: Do not disturb the pleasant surroundings.

Application: Why does a rabbit not eat the grass around its own hole? The rabbit wants to maintain its environment. If it is left untouched, it appears very green and natural. Attention is not called to the area or to the hole.

The saying, "A rabbit does not eat the grass around its own hole", is a metaphor. The word "grass" indicates our close associations. These associations include our relatives, friends, neighbors, and more. Like the rabbit, we need to keep our nearby grass undisturbed. This means that we should be careful to not disturb our pleasant surroundings by maintaining our important relationships. The following story provides an example of this.

I worked at an international firm for ten years. Due to intense competition, the firm decided to lay-off some employees, and I was one of the employees to leave the firm. After telling this news to some of my friends, one friend offered me a job, and I agreed to take it. Once I became an employee, I sensed a great difference in our relationship. We had treated each other equally prior to this employment. Now the attitude of this friend had changed, the manner and the tone of voice were different. I did not want to be treated as his inferior, and I wanted to maintain our friendship as it had been. I kindly resigned after three months. Today, we still communicate with each other and my pleasant surroundings are not disturbed.

Chinese proverb: xian li hou bing.

先礼后兵。

Translation: Apply force only after the diplomatic method has failed.

Meaning: Use courteous methods first, then take strong measures.

Application: This proverb provides a strategy for dealing with tough situations. This strategy appeared first in the Chinese novel *Romance of the Three Kingdoms*. Back then, the tactics were used for diplomatic purposes. Today, we can employ the same tactics to our own human relationships.

The strategy is very simple. It specifies the use of two methods of dealing with others in tough situations. We must first be calm, polite and courteous. This method will be successful most of the time. If this method fails, we will have to use the second method and be very strong.

In life, we must deal with a wide variety of individuals. Some of them will be easy to get along and others will be very unpleasant to deal with. Some people, it seems, are always against us. What should we do? We must first be calm, kind and diplomatic. If that fails, then we need to switch our tactics. We may well be dealing with the type of people who can be described as "bullying the meek and fearing the strong". In this case, we must let them know that we can be very strong. The old saying, "Talk softly and carry a big stick", may be appropriate. Being strong may be the best response to an unreasonable request.

Chinese proverb: xin you ling xi yi dian tong.

心有灵犀一点通。

Translation: An intelligent heart understands by a little tap.

Meaning: Understand others without a word.

Application: Reviewing the Chinese characters in this proverb can help us to understand its meaning. The first four characters of the proverb indicate that the human heart contains the capability of quick and sharp response of a rhinoceros. Chinese people believe that the rhinoceros is a very intelligent animal and that the large and small horns of this animal allow it to quickly sense and understand many things. The following three characters of this proverb indicate understanding by a little tap.

The English interpretation of this proverb is: "Some people can understand the intention of other individuals without needing words or an explanation."

The Chinese typically use this proverb to describe an individual who can understand another individual's heart. Two examples where this proverb is used are shown below. The first example is of a love relationship and the second example is related to learning.

When two people are really in love, they will know each other's heart. The result of this heart knowledge is that verbal communication sometimes may become unnecessary. The two individuals can understand the thoughts of one another without uttering a single word.

In a classroom or at the work place, we sometime can know other people's intention even without their explanation. This happened to me once when I was yet an apprentice in China. My trainer wanted to tell me something, and I understood what this trainer was going to say. Therefore, the trainer stated this proverb to me to point out that I knew what to do already without any explanation.

Chinese proverb: yan duo bi shi.

言多必失。

Translation: Speak too much will leak unnecessary information.

Meaning: Wordiness is not helpful.

Application: This proverb states that wordiness is not helpful. If we speak too much, we will definitely leak unnecessary information. This leaked information may harm us instead of helping us. If you have not yet experienced what this proverb states, that is very good. Most people, however, have had the experience of speaking too much.

Let us suppose that you are engaged in a conversation with someone. After you have made your point, you just keep talking. Your extra words may well have given away some information which could be unfavorable to you. In the meantime, your lengthy words could have caused the hearer to feel very bored.

There is a Chinese saying regarding talking too much, "Once a word is spoken, it cannot be overtaken by a team of four horses." The rule is to speak less and to listen more. If you can remember this simple rule, then you will never leak unnecessary information anymore.

Chinese proverb: yuan qin bu ru jin lin.

远亲不如近邻。

Translation: Nearby neighbors are better than far away relatives.

Meaning: Be kind to your neighbors.

Application: Nearby neighbors are much more important to us than our relatives who live far away. When we need immediate help, our long-distance relatives for sure cannot help us. This proverb teaches a very good concept. Building good friendly relationships with our neighbors is very important.

I can give you my personal experience of how much my neighbor helped me in time of need. When I needed immediate help, my nearby neighbor saved me.

One morning, I was ready to go to work; however, I could not start my car. It was due to my car battery drained overnight. At that time, I lived in the countryside and no public transportation was available. I neither had a working vehicle nor public transportation. To me this was equivalent to saying that I had no "feet", and I desperately needed help! During that particular morning hour, nobody was usually around. Most people were gone either to school or to work already. I was a college instructor, and I had students waiting for me in the classroom. Oh, what should I do?

Fortunately, a neighbor who lived across the street from me happened to be at home. She gave my car a quick jump, and then my car started. I even went to work on time that day. You can imagine how grateful I was for the help I received from my nearby neighbor.

The concept of "Nearby neighbors are better than far away relatives" is perfectly applicable. This incident points out that people should be kind to their neighbors, and they need to help each other.

Chinese proverb: zhi ren zhi mian bu zhi xin.

知人知面不知心。

Translation: You may know the person and the person's face, but not the person's heart.

Meaning: You do not actually know the person.

Application: As expressed in other proverbs, it takes time and effort to truly know the heart of other human beings. You believe that you know certain people very well. In actual fact, you may not know them at all. The following story reminds us why we need to be cautious.

Betty wanted to share exciting news with her best friend, Joan. She invited Joan over for a nice dinner. At the dinner, Betty told her friend that she was engaged and would soon be married. A few days later, Betty introduced her fiancé to Joan. After this, Betty had trouble contacting her fiancé. Soon Betty received the absolutely shocking news that her best friend, Joan, and her fiancé got married.

Betty never had any suspicion that her best friend might do this. The news was such a heavy blow to Betty and it completely shattered her entire being. Her heart was so sad that eventually Betty became mentally ill. Betty never got married, and she left the world at a rather young age with the illness.

We should ask ourselves a question, "Do we really know the heart of our close friends?" We need to meditate on this for a few minutes. Before I leave this page, I would like to pen a positive note. It is probably unlike the story above; each of your close friends is very honest and loyal.

CHAPTER 9

Society

Chinese proverb: an fen shou ji.

安分守己。

Translation: Abide by the law and behave yourself.

Meaning: Obey the rules and keep tranquility.

Application: A Ming dynasty poet witnessed human behavior that, to his convictions, were unethical. He then wrote a poem using this proverb to give advice to the Chinese people. The purpose of his poem was to urge Chinese people to abide by the law and behave themselves. Although it has been over three hundred years from the Ming dynasty to the present time, the advice is still applicable today.

Throughout history, there have been two types of human behaviors. One type is sound and the other type is contrary to correct conduct. The Ming poet considered heavy drinking, pornography, greed, and dishonesty to be very destructive to a society. The poet believed that people who behaved themselves in such a way would harm not just others but also themselves.

After several hundred years, the poet's point is still valid today. Whatever was harmful in the past is still harmful today; and whatever was beneficial in the past is still beneficial today. If we agree with the view of this proverb, then we should abide by the law and behave ourselves.

Chinese proverb: bi jue feng qing.

弊绝风清。

Translation: Remove evil to establish a clean society.

Meaning: Clean up society.

Application: According to this proverb, human society should be clean from corruption. When a society is filled with iniquities, then it is time for cleaning. We can relate cleansing society to our own house spring-cleaning.

How do we clean our house in the spring? We normally will get rid of the unnecessary stuff first. After we throw away the clutter, we then can thoroughly clean everywhere. We sweep, mop, and wash, etc. Sometimes we even repaint the entire house. It is a big effort. After all of the effort we put in, the house will have a very clean new look. Similarly, if we and other people make a very big effort to clean up society together, society will have a fresh new look as well.

Chinese proverb: bing qiang ma zhuang.

兵强马壮。

Translation: Soldiers are strong, and horses are sturdy.

Meaning: The protection of a society is from the armed forces.

Application: This proverb indicates that a society must equip itself with powerful armed forces. If we look around, we can see that almost every nation in this world has armed forces. Every society needs protection, and the protection comes from armed forces.

We know that strong and powerful armed forces will protect their people from foreign invasions. When society has peace, then citizens can have security. Peace and security then can produce prosperity.

Chinese proverb: chun lan qiu ju.

春兰秋菊。

Translation: Spring has orchids and autumn has chrysanthemums.

Meaning: Each season has its own beauty.

Application: This proverb is an analogy. It uses flowers of two different seasons (i.e., spring and autumn) to indicate that each season holds its very own attractiveness. Spring has beautiful orchids; autumn has lovely chrysanthemums. The natural beauty is very easy to see. Yet if we look at it slightly deeper, we will understand that the proverb is pointing out something more meaningfully.

The beauty which this proverb expresses describes each individual in society. Just like the spring orchids and autumn chrysanthemums, each holds its own special charm; likewise, each person in society possesses his or her very own unique and special qualities as well. All of these unique and special qualities of individuals combine together to create a multifaceted, interesting, functional and beautiful society.

Chinese proverb: du mu bu cheng lin.

独木不成林。

Translation: A lone tree cannot become a forest.

Meaning: One single tree has its limitation.

Application: A single tree cannot form a forest, and a forest is full of many individual trees. We can reflect on that idea. When a huge windstorm comes, one tree will be blown down. Together, many trees can protect each other and withstand the storm.

Similarly, a single person is not a society. A society is made up of many individuals with all kinds of skills and capabilities. A single person may be destroyed by calamity while a society can overcome the calamity. In a society, people provide help and support to one another. A society which is filled with skilled and caring people will be splendid with great capabilities.

Chinese proverb: feng tiao yu shun.

風調雨順。

Translation: The wind and rain are cooperating.

Meaning: It is very pleasant.

Application: This proverb addresses the harmony of wind and rain. When the wind and the rain cooperate with each other, then the weather will be very pleasant. The concept of this proverb applies not only to weather but also to human societies. Human societies will function very well when individuals in the society work together.

When the wind and rain cooperate, they together will create a pleasant and comfortable day. When citizens of a society work well together, then that society can become very harmonious. A harmonious society can make everyone's life peaceable and enjoyable.

Chinese proverb: guo tai min an.

国泰民安。

Translation: Make one's nation peaceful for the public.

Meaning: People feel safe when a nation has peace.

Application: One of the most valuable things which a nation can have is peace. Peace with other countries can be achieved with diplomacy and a strong military. When a nation is at peace, her citizens feel secure and can focus on business, education, the arts and leisure. Peace and prosperity are linked very closely together. History shows us that nations at peace are able to quickly build wealth. King Solomon is an example of this. The country of Israel was at peace during his entire forty-year reign. During that time, both the king and then entire nation became very wealthy.

Chinese proverb: jian shan tian xia.

兼善天下。

Translation: Double the good deeds for the world.

Meaning: Be as twice as kind.

Application: This proverb instructs us to be kind and to do good deeds. We should certainly be kind and remember that when kindness is given, kindness is usually returned to us. The proverb directs us to double the number of good deeds which we think that we should perform.

Let us take a moment to analyze the Chinese characters in this proverb, so that we might have a better comprehension of the meaning. The first character, 兼, indicates double or twice; the following character, 善, designates kindness or compassion. The last two characters, 天下, indicate the world or all people. Evaluating the meanings of the characters lead us to understand that we all should be compassionate, and double kindness to everyone. Therefore, we should perform good deeds whenever possible.

Chinese proverb: zhen tong ren he.

政通人和。

Translation: Affairs of the state are open and clear with people's support.

Meaning: People support their good government.

Application: The description provided by this proverb is one of a government functions in an honest and open manner. A government functions in this manner has nothing to hide. Its books will be open for review and its citizens will support it.

This proverb describes an ideal society. In this world, we have to work with what we have and make it better. People are not faultless. There is an old saying, "Gold cannot be one hundred percent pure; human cannot be one hundred percent perfect." Our government may be far from open and clear. We may keep this proverb in mind and work together to make progress.

CHAPTER 10

Success

Chinese proverb: ang shou kuo bu.

昂首阔步。

Translation: Head is up, and stride is big.

Meaning: An accomplished person acts successfully.

Application: This proverb describes people who have succeeded. Successful individuals do act differently and are positive in outlook on life. The description given in this proverb is one of accomplished individuals with dignified postures. They hold their heads high and their strides are big. This posture reflects inner satisfaction of their success.

Many of us desire to attain success and to accomplish great things. To do this, we will have to think and act differently. We must have a vision of the future. We then must think big and act to make our vision a reality. As stated in the proverb, our head should be up, and our step should be big. This is not just a physical description of our posture but it should also describe our spirit.

Chinese proverb: bai lian cheng gang.

百炼成钢。

Translation: Be tempered into steel after smelting a hundred times.

Meaning: Be strong.

Application: This proverb invokes thoughts of strength and durability. These excellent merits of strength and durability are not gained easily. Just as metal must undergo a smelting process, we also must be refined and strengthened in the refining fire of life.

It takes much effort to create the finest steel. The saying, "Iron can be tempered into steel after smelting a hundred times" might be an exaggeration for steel. However, it is realistic when indicating the smelting process of our characters and soul. The hundreds of challenges, which are a part of human life, are like a refining fire to our characters.

As we go through the smelting process and are changed from iron to steel, our spirit will become as strong as steel. We will be able to overcome all kinds of difficulties and achieve our dreams in life. Therefore, it is indeed necessary for successful people to go through the "smelting" process. In the end, we will become so strong that nothing can stop us from attaining our achievements.

Chinese proverb: bai shou qi jia.

白手起家。

Translation: You are able to build up from nothing.

Meaning: Do not fear difficulties.

Application: Let us first review the characters of this proverb for a better understanding. The first two characters, 白手, indicate empty hands or nothing; then 起家 indicate to build up as in to build up a home or establish an enterprise.

This proverb comes from the Ming dynasty. During that period, the main purpose of this proverb was to encourage people to establish their homes. People could establish their homes even with empty hands.

Today, this proverb can be an encouragement to those of us who wish to create a home or a business. Just as the ancient Chinese believed they could establish their homes with empty hands. Success does not necessary depend upon a large amount of starting capital.

This proverb encourages us and tells us not to fear difficulties. If you have both drive and the diligence, you can succeed. As long as you possess great ambitions and lofty ideas, you will have all that is needed to achieve.

Chinese proverb: ban shi de sheng.

班师得胜。

Translation: The military returned victoriously.

Meaning: The military came back in triumph.

Application: "The military returned victoriously" is a proverb full of rejoicing, praise and renewed hope for the future. Can we transfer this exciting feeling of praise, hope and excitement into our modern life? The answer is yes.

We are fighting daily battles to achieve our goals and dreams. We may lose some of those battles; however, we will often win those battles. When we are triumphant, we should take some time to celebrate and rejoice. If we take time to be thankful for our blessings of victory and accomplishment, our outlook on life will take a turn for the better.

Chinese proverb: bu bai zhi di.

不败之地。

Translation: You stand in an invincible position.

Meaning: It is unbeatable.

Application: A Chinese military genius named Sun Tzu, 孙子, wrote a very famous book called *The Art of War*. The book was written during the Spring and Autumn period (771-476 BC). This book which deals with strategies and tactics for military warfare was the source of this proverb. *The Art of War* has been studied for over 1,500 years and is currently used in military schools and read by many individuals throughout the world.

This proverb describes a position which is very favorable. It is an unconquerable or invincible position. If you place yourself in such a position, success is highly likely. How can you put yourself in this invincible position? My advice is to read and study *The Art of War*. It contains a wealth of valuable knowledge which you can put to use in present day situations. I believe gaining knowledge is a great advantage in working to achieve success. I also believe that to be successful, you must have an unbeatable spirit residing deep down in your soul. That unconquerable spirit is the most important element of all for attaining success.

Chinese proverb: bu bu deng gao.

步步登高。

Translation: Rise higher with each step.

Meaning: Climb up steadily.

Application: "Rise higher with each step" is one definition of successful individuals. The proverb implies that a consistent movement in an upward direction. If you can learn to climb up steadily, you will become a great achiever. The upward steps are easier to take if you first set up your goals and then create a blueprint showing the steps you want to take in your life. When you follow your blueprint carefully, you will rise higher with each step.

Chinese proverb: bu ru hu xue, yan de hu zi.

不入虎穴,焉得虎子。

Translation: If you do not get into tiger's den, you cannot catch tiger cubs.

Meaning: Success may require taking risks.

Application: Would you like to become a very successful individual? If your answer is yes, then you must be a risk taker. This is because success requires taking chances. If you look around, you will see that not too many people are enormously prosperous. Why is this the case? The answer is that most people are not risk takers.

Once we understand the reality of the need for taking risks to achieve success, we will begin to act differently to achieve success. We may even get into tiger's den to catch the tiger's cubs.

Chinese proverb: da gong gao cheng.

大功告成。

Translation: One performed an exceptionally praiseworthy mission.

Meaning: A person has accomplished remarkably.

Application: This proverb gives praise to individuals who have performed outstanding missions. I feel that there are two categories of these terrific people. One group is made up of extraordinarily famous individuals. The other group is made up of millions of people who are unknown to the world.

The truth could be that individuals from both groups are equally important, whether they are well known or unknown. The famous individuals are already known by the world and therefore I would like to emphasize the accomplishments of those who are unknown to the world. Individuals, from the unknown group who have given their best, truly deserve our praise. What missions are truly praiseworthy? This depends on the individual. To some, a praiseworthy mission might be the graduation from college. To others, it may be to the creation of a business. The exact nature of the praiseworthy mission is not as important as the fact that they gave their very best to complete the extremely difficult mission.

The following story can be an inspiration to us. This individual in the story is one of millions who are unknown to the world; however, his achievement is almost equal to those are celebrated worldwide. The purpose of telling this story is to encourage everyone who has tried or is still trying.

My youngest child, Daniel, was born with a cognitive learning disability. As the years advanced, he faced tremendous challenges in learning. Like many people in this world, he enjoyed music immensely. He admired other people who could play piano and wanted to take piano lessons.

Several piano teachers refused to take a student who was born with a cognitive difficulty. They did not believe Daniel could ever learn to play piano. The rejections almost broke my heart. Due to having an exceptionally loving nature, Daniel did not let the rejections affect him.

Finally, a genuinely kindhearted piano teacher took Daniel as a student. (It is a comforting truth to know that there are many sympathetic human beings in this world). After years of diligently learning and practicing piano, Daniel has become remarkably accomplished in playing the piano. Today, Daniel can play Hymns, Christmas music, and some folk music.

Chinese proverb: li shen yang ming.

立身扬名。

Translation: Establish a well-known social status.

Meaning: Individuals can attain popularity.

Application: If you would like to make a name for yourself, it may well be possible if you follow the advice of this proverb. Attaining popularity might actually be a very positive thing for you to do. According to this ancient Chinese proverb, if an individual would like to attain popularity, he or she must first develop the correct internal moral character.

Reviewing the characters in this proverb can help with our understanding. The first two characters of this proverb, 立身, indicate setting up a process of self-cultivation; the last two characters, 扬名, designate becoming famous. Based on the teaching of this proverb, therefore, individuals need to cultivate their moral character first, and then they may successfully achieve fame and a high social status.

The idea of the proverb is to teach people the correct method of attaining social status and recognition. The correct method is to first improve one's self through self-cultivation, and then rise in fame and popularity through selfless service. Establishing social status is not intended for self-gain, but rather, it is to contribute for the benefit of the public. Popularity and social recognition should only arrive after a person has performed contributions focused on others.

We now live in the twenty-first century, and this ancient philosophy may seem outdated. You also might not wish to be popular or have a high social status. My hope is that if you agree with the philosophy of this proverb, you can begin to cultivate a very positive moral character within yourself. After you have gone through a period of self-cultivation, you may become popular and enjoy the popularity.

Chinese proverb: shui dao qu cheng.

水到渠成。

Translation: Where water flows, a channel is formed.

Meaning: When conditions are ripe, success will come.

Application: "Where water flows, a channel is formed." The word "water" in this statement represents a required condition, and the word "channel" signifies success. With the water flow, there will be the formation of the channel. Therefore, when conditions are ripe, obtaining the desired achievement is possible and easy.

The meaning of this proverb is "When conditions are ripe, success will come". Therefore, this proverb can be used by individuals who want to be successful. Many of the Chinese proverbs in this book can help to motivate people toward accomplishment. This proverb in particular can help you to achieve success without any problems.

Conditions can become ripe at any time and without us doing much work. Therefore, there will always be potential fulfillment. Let's use agriculture as an example to help us see the meaning of the proverb plainly. When apples are ripe, apple pickers will find it very easy to pick a basket full of apples. In the spring season, if you plant cucumber seeds in the soil, you can harvest your juicy cucumbers after a little over two months.

Chinese proverb: qi kai de sheng.

旗开得胜。

Translation: Raise the flag and claim the victory.

Meaning: Success is at hand.

Application: In the Chinese language, this proverb literally states that when you raise the flag, you will have the victory. The proverb implies that success is guaranteed.

At a high level, this proverb is teaching us to trust ourselves. That is, once we have studied a situation, we need to fully trust in our judgement and act without hesitation or fear. This proverb is true and effective, however, to obtain the guaranteed success, you must wipe out all the negative thoughts in your heart. Indeed, success begins within your own heart. If your heart can truly believe that success is at hand, then you certainly can succeed! Deep down in your heart, you must have a very positive outlook. Do not ponder the obstacles to be overwhelmed. Do not think that the proverb is too easy to be true or too simple. You need to confidently remind yourself and believe within that "Success is at hand".

Let us suppose you are about to start a new business venture. You might have two different thoughts regarding the future of the venture. One thought could be fear of failure. Letting this fear into your heart may well lead you to failure. On the other hand, however, you might be completely confident of success. According to this proverb, your one hundred percent confidence will lead you to success. This is what "Raise the flag and claim the victory" all about.

Chinese proverb: xiao bu ren ze luan da mou.

小不忍则乱大谋。

Translation: One must tolerate small humiliations to carry out important missions.

Meaning: Forbearance absolutely is necessary.

Application: Forbearance absolutely is necessary. To forbear is to restrain. As human beings, we do not enjoy restraining ourselves. Nevertheless, according to Chinese philosophy, forbearance is unquestionably essential. It is particularly essential to those who wish to attain great success.

If we want to carry out an important mission, we must tolerate many small humiliations. No great work has ever been accomplished without small humiliations. Tolerance and self-control are virtues. To accomplish important missions and to improve ourselves with virtue, we must tolerate some humiliation.

Let us consider an application of this proverb. For many years, the building of a canal across the isthmus of Panama had been a dream. The French extended great effort into the building of this canal and failed. One of the greatest challenges was that large numbers of men died from the tropical diseases of yellow fever and malaria. When the United States began their efforts to construct the canal, they knew that they would have many setbacks and humiliations, however, they determined to endure and succeed. A Colonel named William Crawford Gorgas was placed in charge of hospitals and sanitation. Colonel Gorgas believed that mosquitoes were carriers of the tropical diseases and he set out to eradicate them by destroying their breeding grounds. The great success of building of the Panama Canal by the United states, came at the expense of many large and small humiliations. If you have a big mission to be fulfilled, then you absolutely need to remember the teaching of this proverb.

Chinese proverb: xing xing zhi huo, ke yi liao yuan.

星星之火,可以燎原。

Translation: A tiny spark may set the whole prairie ablaze.

Meaning: Insignificant ventures may develop into enormous success.

Application: It is true that a very tiny spark may set the whole prairie ablaze. If you have never experienced this, you most likely have heard of it occurring. Thinking of just a tiny spark growing to be the raging flames of whole prairie is almost unimaginable!

Now let us consider how to apply this concept in our own lives. We are completing our chapter about success, and this proverb can certainly assist us in the areas of achievement and success. Suppose you just began an insignificant business venture. You work very diligently and very wisely on the venture, and the small business keeps growing steadily. It then grows into a huge accomplishment.

This proverb can describe an entrepreneur I personally know. This person began a very small venture related to customized boat motors in a garage. The business has now developed into a very successful company providing employment to many. A tiny spark may set the whole prairie ablaze; a small venture may develop into an enormous success.

CHAPTER 11

Wealth

Chinese proverb: ai cai ru ming.

爱财如命。

Translation: A person can love wealth as much as his life.

Meaning: People care too much about their money.

Application: "People care too much about their money" gives a negative image of misers of the world. Although some of us may not want to deal with them; however, we can analyze this proverb in both positive and negative ways.

Let us analyze the positive side first. Money does not fall from the sky into people's hands. It comes to people in a number of ways. Most people work very hard to earn their income. As the result of industrious work, people need to be wise with their money. Some people try to save up as much of their earned income as possible, which can be seen as a positive thing. Our human nature tells us that almost every person treasures wealth because of the possibilities that wealth can afford.

On the other hand, if a person begins to love that money above all else, it will likely create problems. It can adversely affect relationships a person has with everyone in his life, including his family members. I would like to share a story with you in the following paragraph.

I had an uncle who really treasured his money. He lived in a lovely home and he lacked nothing. However, he could hardly stand his relatives to dine with him. We occasionally visited him and ate at his house. However, every time the dishes clinked, he felt uneasy. When his children needed financial help, he would always refuse to help them. Even though he was wealthy, he lived a very thrifty life. At his death, he left a huge amount of money behind.

We cannot take anything with us. Some people may temporarily possess enormous wealth; however, those individuals can never ultimately have real control of their possessions. After their departure, their wealth merely transfers to the hands of other individuals.

Then, why should we be greedy? If we knew today was our last day on earth, we would stop accumulating possessions and wealth. We may want to live today as if it were our last day on earth. If that were the case, we would live today with real meaning, and we would not care too much about money. If we can truly comprehend life and wealth, then we will live with a sensible balance.

Chinese proverb: chi chou wo suan.

持筹握算。

Translation: One plans and makes keen decisions in finance.

Meaning: Manage finances astutely.

Application: This proverb teaches people a very clever method of handling money. An ingenious financial person knows exactly the inflow and outflow of money, and this person will never allow the outflow of money to be greater than its inflow.

The following example will demonstrate some financial issues that could be fall a person. Suppose you have a $7,000 income monthly, and your monthly expense total $7,200. If you keep this pattern, you for sure would create a financial disaster for yourself.

I know two individuals whose backgrounds and income were very similar. One of them retired at the age of 42; the other individual still has to work at age of 66. How can that be? The truth is that retirement is not an issue of age but rather an issue of money. The person who retired at 42 knew the theory of this proverb, and he practiced the theory to the core. On the contrary, the other person did not know how to manage his finances astutely. As a result, he could have only one choice regarding retirement—to work in perpetuity.

Chinese proverb: chi zhuo bu jin.

吃著不尽。

Translation: You have more than enough for food and clothing.

Meaning: A privileged position removes financial concerns.

Application: This proverb originally comes from the Song dynasty. During that period, those who wanted to serve the emperor had to take imperial examinations. Those who could pass the examinations with excellent scores would be appointed to various official positions to serve the emperor. In one of such assessments, an important member of the Imperial Academy teased the scholar who had the highest marks in the highest imperial examination. This member said to the winner, "You will have more than enough for food and clothing from now on." The winner proudly replied, "My desire was in the study; I am not interested in food and clothing."

Regardless of the real motive of the winner, the scholar who won the first place in the highest imperial examination unquestionably would receive wealth and rank. According to Chinese history, an emperor normally let his daughter marry the scholar who had the highest marks in the highest imperial examination.

Chinese proverb: chuo chuo you yu.

绰绰有余。

Translation: It is more than sufficient.

Meaning: Have enough to spare.

Application: Perhaps most people in this world would like to have more than sufficient. People who actually have more than enough to spare can live without any financial difficulties. Yet the fact is that the majority of living beings in this world are not at that level. Therefore, if you want to reach the level of more than sufficient, then you need to have a very good financial plan.

A friend of mine once mentioned to me a financial plan for living an abundant life. This plan is very simple; however, it requires discipline. More precisely, this financial plan is the 60/40 ratio plan.

My friend believed that people should have 60 percent of their monthly income as expenditure, and save 40 percent into their savings. The friend of mine, in fact, lived very abundantly. Her life of having enough to spare was because she did exactly what she believed. If you follow the plan of the 60/40 ratio plan, you will for sure have more than sufficient.

Chinese proverb: di shui cheng he.

滴水成河。

Translation: Each drop of water can accumulate to form a river.

Meaning: A little effort may amount to be enormous.

Application: If people believe a little effort may amount to be enormous, then this proverb certainly makes sense. The teaching here is incontestably valuable for every person. Therefore, you may use the principle in your own savings. If you continually save a small amount of money, then you will eventually be able to accumulate a huge quantity. Each insignificant amount you put aside may someday completely surprise you.

You can nod your head about the notion of this proverb. It is because the principle is indeed valid and encouraging. If tiny drops of water can accumulate to become a river, so can people regularly save small amounts of money to grow into a large quantity. Nevertheless, to every good principle there must be a commitment. Without any exception, this precise principle requires people's commitment. When you can discipline yourself and make effort, you may have your tiny steady savings accumulate into huge wealth someday.

Chinese proverb: jian bu xu fa.

箭不虚发。

Translation: Never shoot an arrow without a target.

Meaning: Do not be wasteful.

Application: If you shoot an arrow without a target, the arrow is wasted. Naturally, it is not a good practice. Therefore, this proverb would have us to never be wasteful in anything. If an athlete never shoots an arrow without a target, then this athlete will not waste the arrow. Since this chapter is about wealth, you perhaps can apply the concept of "Never shoot an arrow without a target" in finance.

From the finance point of view, you may substitute arrows for dollars. If one arrow is one dollar, then you can comprehend the meaning of this proverb clearly. Suppose you are in a mood for expenditure and you spend your dollar without any real purpose; as a result, your dollar of course is wasted. According to the teaching of this proverb, you shoot your "arrow" without a target. On the other hand, if you keep your dollar and you spend it when there is a need, the dollar is used rationally.

I know an individual who is a financial consultant. This person mentioned to me that he would always try to save a dollar without spending it unreasonably. He then gave me one of his examples: If I have a five-dollar bill in my wallet, I would keep the money without wasting it on things such as a can of soft drink, a bag of chips, etc. The five-dollar bill would be safely tucked in my wallet.

You perhaps will wonder why this financial consultant tried to save his money as small as one five-dollar bill. The reason is very simple. Being a wise financial consultant, he must never shoot his "arrow" with an empty target. When his clients wanted to consult with him, he could be consciously aware that he himself had set a good example already, so that he could provide correct solutions.

Chinese proverb: kai yuan jie liu.

开源节流。

Translation: Open up resources and cut down expenditures.

Meaning: Broaden sources of income and reduce expenses.

Application: This proverb appears simple and yet it is very powerful. If one meditates on it and employs its principles in life, it will likely make that individual very wealthy. Let us take a quick look at its two components.

The first component is to open up resources; it focuses on income. We should always look for ways to increase income. This includes a wide variety of possibilities. We can do better at our jobs, start new businesses, learn to invest and invent new ways of making money. The possibilities are endless.

The second component is equally important to the first. This component is to cut down expenditures. When expenditures exceed income, one becomes poor. When income exceeds expenditures, one becomes financially well off. When we use our imagination, many opportunities to save money come to mind. From small to large, we have multiple options. Eating out less, paying off your house early and not going into credit card debt are very important. Living simply and beneath your means now will lead to financial freedom in the future.

Chinese proverb: sheng cai you dao.

生财有道。

Translation: One has a method of making money.

Meaning: Certain people have a way to increase their wealth.

Application: This proverb implies that some people were born with a talent to increase their wealth. If you happen to be one of them, you should feel very fortunate about yourself. It is because not every person in this world was born that way. If you were not born with a talent to increase your wealth, you can learn to become one. It absolutely is not an issue. Many people around the world who want to become financially free take related trainings. If you keep learning and practicing what you learned, you can also obtain the skill to be prosperous.

Chinese proverb: yi ben wan li.

一本万利。

Translation: A small investment may bring a ten-thousand-fold profit.

Meaning: Good fortune may start by investing wisely.

Application: People can make great fortune by investing wisely. Sometimes people can profit big with a small capital. Is it possible? Yes, it is possible. If you research on wealthy people, you will find out that some of them harvested good fortunes by merely making small investments.

This proverb may give you an idea concerning very clever investments. You perhaps think that people can work harder to make extra income. For that reason, people do not need to invest at all. You certainly have a valid point. It is true that people must work hard to make a living. However, if people desire to live a very comfortable life, then they will likely need to invest. Astute investments can bring good fortunes. Hence, if you desire wealth for your life, you might want to get into investments. If that defines you, then you need to do two things: education and action.

First, you need to learn about various types of investments. Once you have learned the strategies of what and how, the next step for you is action. Without action, nothing will happen. People can have great investment plans; however, their plans will do nothing until they execute their plans. Education and action go hand in hand. Who knows, you may bring a ten thousand fold profit with a small investment amount.

Chinese proverb: yin xiao shi da.

因小失大。

Translation: One suffered a big loss only for a small profit.

Meaning: Lose big for small gain.

Application: To suffer a big loss only for a small profit is certainly not a wise thing to do. Nobody will intentionally suffer big losses only for small profits. However, sometimes people do profit small and lose big by mistake. Even though mistakes are painful, they can teach people a lesson.

Insightful business people typically plan to make considerable profits. It is the intention of any business to make gain. Therefore, if you want to make profit, you need to calculate the ratio of gain and loss prior to committing financially. If you do your homework and estimate correctly, you can make it much more likely that you have good returns and avoid unnecessary losses.

Chinese proverb: ying you jin you.

应有尽有。

Translation: Everything that you expect to get you have already.

Meaning: You lack nothing at all.

Application: Most people would agree that they would like to live a marvelous life on earth. While what is marvelous may differ from person to person, most people would agree that if they could have everything they desire, that would amount to a marvelous life. In other words, if you could only lack nothing at all, life would be perfect. What a dream it would be if you could have anything you wanted to have. This proverb portrays people whose life style is extremely incredible. Can you think of individuals you personally know that actually live such an incredible life? You may shake your head because you cannot think of anyone who lacks nothing at all, least of all you yourself.

However, you can relate this proverb to a very famous king. King Solomon was exceptionally wealthy. When he was alive, he had everything he desired. He had more money than he could ever use, seven hundred wives and three hundred concubines, and he was beloved by his people. Therefore, King Solomon would seem to be a quite apt illustration of this proverb. King Solomon wrote a book called Ecclesiastes, which reveals his innermost thoughts on his seemingly splendid life.

The following quotation is from Ecclesiastes 2:10-11: "Whatever my eyes desired I did not keep from them. I did not withhold my heart from any pleasure, For my heart rejoiced in all my labor; And this was my reward from all my labor. Then I looked on all the works that my hands had done and on the labor in which I had toiled; And indeed all was vanity and grasping for the wind. There was no profit under the sun."

After King Solomon obtained everything his heart had desired, and he had lived an exceedingly indulgent life, he considered all he had and all he had accomplished to be vanity. He did not describe his life as marvelous or perfect, but rather as vanity, or pointless.

Therefore, having everything you desire may not lead to a perfect life. Surely, getting everything your heart desires can temporary make you extremely satisfied. However, that satisfaction may not last very long. The truth would seem to be that while successes and material possessions may grant temporary happiness, however, true happiness is not found in these things. Now, you may meditate upon the definition of true happiness.

Chinese proverb: zheng zheng ri shang.

蒸蒸日上。

Translation: Steam goes up higher and higher daily.

Meaning: Your wealth will continue to grow more and more.

Application: First, you may spend a few minutes to analyze the Chinese characters of this proverb. The first two characters of this proverb point to "steam", and the following two characters indicate "going up every day". Steam will always evaporate toward the sky. Therefore, if you picture steam in your mind, you can imagine it going up higher and higher.

This proverb states a figurative language. It actually indicates the phenomenon of prosperity. Hence, you can apply this proverb to describe the prosperity of nations, businesses, families, or individuals. Similarly, if you are pleased with your life, you can certainly think of your life as the steam goes up higher and higher every day. In other words, your wealth will continue to grow.

CHAPTER 12

Miscellaneous

Chinese proverb: an bu jiu ban.

安部就班。

Translation: Follow the conventional ways of doing things.

Meaning: Do things according to established regulations

Application: The advice of this proverb points us toward doing things according to the set regulations. This can be found to be pure common sense. For example, if the regular business hours of your company are from eight o'clock to five o'clock (including one hour for lunch), then you and other employees need to be there at eight in the morning and leave at five in the late afternoon. This is the conventional way of doing things.

Chinese proverb: an shen li ming.

安身立命。

Translation: Settle down and start your life.

Meaning: Do not drift.

Application: "Settle down and start your life" is a good recommendation for people of all ages. However, this recommendation is particularly suitable to young people. People who are young have many advantages. One of those advantages could be that they have plenty of time ahead. For that reason, some of them will wander around, perhaps searching for their ideal job or an ideal life. They believe that once they find what they desire, they will settle down.

As young people, they definitely have the right idea. Nevertheless, if it continues and becomes a habit, they could waste their life drifting. It is not a good thing to be constantly wandering. This habit causes many to not live up to their own potential. Even without the habit of wandering, most of people will not find a perfect life on this planet. Wandering, however, reduces your chances for happiness considerably. If people settle down and focus on their goals as early as possible, then their life can be full of promise.

Chinese proverb: bai wen bu ru yi jian.

百闻不如一见。

Translation: It is better to see once than to hear a hundred times.

Meaning: Seeing is believing.

Application: This is a very straightforward saying. People, in general, believe what they see rather than what they hear. Therefore, you will agree that while it is difficult for others to persuade you with words, when they actually show things which you can see with your own eyes, you can readily accept them as truth. In other words, seeing is believing.

Chinese proverb: bai zhi hei zi.

白纸黑字。

Translation: A white sheet of paper has black inked words.

Meaning: It is solid evidence.

Application: This proverb defines solid evidence. It uses a white sheet of paper that containing words in black ink to emphasize hard evidence. What does this proverb try to tell you? It tries to inform you that you need to be very cautious about what you write to other people.

At a company where I worked, one of the office workers wrote an email to anther office worker. The person who received the email showed it to her supervisor. The next day, the supervisor called the person who wrote the email to her office and fired the individual. Remember that a word written is like a rock thrown. They both are difficult to retrieve.

Chinese proverb: ban men nong fu.

班门弄斧。

Translation: People demonstrate their carpentry skills before the master carpenter.

Meaning: It is foolish to display one's slight skill before an expert.

Application: According to Chinese history, there once lived a highly skilled carpenter, whose name was Lu Ban. Lu Ban's carpentry skill was so proficient that no other contemporary carpenters could match his skill. If any carpenter claimed that his carpentry skill surpassed Lu Ban's, people would consider the man to be just a boaster. From Lu Ban's time forward, Chinese people use this proverb to indicate either foolishness or arrogance.

Arrogance is a fault in people. Chinese people believe that the opposite to this fault is modesty. Modest people do not boast or show off. On the contrary, they are humble and just let their deeds speak for themselves.

Chinese proverb: ban qi shi tou za zi ji de jiao.

搬起石头砸自己的脚。

Translation: One picks up a rock and hits one's own feet.

Meaning: One harms one's self.

Application: This proverb is a warning signal to all people. The warning is that if any person desires to harm others, that person may very likely hurt himself instead. There is a Divine Justice ruling the universe and this proverb is often seen to be true. If people devise evil plans toward others, they very well might become the recipient of their own plan.

Chinese proverb: bu yuan tian, bu you ren.

不怨天，不尤人。

Translation: Do not complain either to heaven or to people.

Meaning: Take responsibility.

Application: People need to be responsible for their own actions. When people make mistakes, they often point their finger at others. They do not want to be accountable for their mistakes.

Helen and Joe were neighborhood friends. From the early days of childhood, they played together and enjoyed each other's company. When Helen reached her early twenties, she wanted to date. Over a period of three years, she had several blind dates also dated men from her work. Helen did not believe that any of these men was the right partner for her, and she started complaining. Helen thought that her friends and her parents had set up wrong blind dates and had not helped her to find the right person.

Joe, meanwhile, had been watching quietly on the side. When Helen one day complained to him of her problems, Joe had the love and courage to ask her for a date. Helen all of a sudden realized that she had loved Joe from childhood. Not long after their initial date, they got married.

Chinese proverb: cheng ren zhi mei.

成人之美。

Translation: Help others to succeed.

Meaning: Assist people to fulfill their dreams.

Application: Perhaps most people would agree that helping others to succeed is an honorable thing to do. However, few of us actually do what this proverb teaches. People are naturally selfish, however, some noble individuals do have unselfish sentiments.

I was told a true story regarding this proverb. In the early twentieth century, there was a certain poor young peasant who lived in China. His parents were poor, and he did not have the opportunity to go to school. Even though this young man was very bright, his dream of obtaining an education was beyond his reach. The young man believed that he would be a poor peasant all of his life.

However, his opportunity came very suddenly. One day, while he was about to begin tilling the field, his landowner happened to meet him face-to-face. The landowner looked at the young man, and then he said to himself, "This young man seems very bright. Why should this bright person till the fields all of his life?" The landowner's heart filled with genuine compassion for the poor man, and he decided to help him. He was convinced that the young man should have the opportunity to go to school. From that moment on, the landowner treated the young peasant as if he were his own son, and the poor peasant's destiny was forever changed.

The kindhearted landowner did perform the noble thing he believed in. He sent the young peasant to school and spent a huge amount of his own fortune to make the young man succeed. In response, the young man worked hard to be worthy of his benefactor's kindness. He studied diligently at school, and in the end, the young man became a scholar. The landowner was extremely happy to see the poor peasant succeed.

The story reminds us that noble people do exist in this world. If we are kind and selfless like that landowner, we can seize opportunities to assist others in fulfilling their dreams. By assisting other individuals to live up to their potentials, we will truly become worthy human beings.

Chinese proverb: chi yi qian zhang yi zhi.

吃一堑长一智。

Translation: Fall into a pit, gain in your wit.

Meaning: Learn from one's own mistakes.

Application: "A pit" stated above represents a mistake. Mistakes, big or small, can be painful. To avoid the pain, we need to avoid making mistakes. As humans, we cannot always make perfect decisions and sometimes we will fall into a pit.

There is only one good thing that I can say about falling into a pit. It is that we are given "wit" or the opportunity to learn from our own mistakes. Learning from our mistakes is a good thing, it enables us to avoid falling into the same pit in the future.

Chinese proverb: chong ru bu jing.

宠辱不惊。

Translation: Keep the same manner whether one receives favor or shame.

Meaning: Remain indifferent whether granted favors or subject to humiliation.

Application: This proverb teaches the importance of retaining our human dignity. Most individuals will act one way when praise and another way when humiliated. The humiliation or disgrace mentioned here is not about individuals having done something wrong or committing a crime. Rather, it is that people are in a receiving position without much control.

We should strive to always be composed and self-controlled. There should only be a slight variation in our demeanor when favored or shamed. We should be thankful and composed when favored; quiet and composed when humiliated.

Chinese proverb: chu kou shang ren.

出口伤人。

Translation: Open your mouth to hurt people.

Meaning: It is wrong to speak unkindly.

Application: We may hurt others with words when our hearts are filled with anger or when we are miserable. If this is the case, we must calm ourselves down.

A piano teacher once told me that playing the piano gives the player several wonderful benefits. One of these benefits is that the player's emotions and feelings are expressed through the music. Distressed hearts are soothed, and rough emotions are calmed.

Not everyone in the world can play musical instruments, however, everyone can sing! The human voice is the best musical instrument of all. Therefore, when you are frustrated, or you burn with anger, you should take time to sing. Singing wholeheartedly can express your frustration and rage. After that, you may become yourself again.

Chinese proverb: ci di wu yin san bai liang.

此地无银三百两。

Translation: There is no three hundred ounces of silver here.

Meaning: The intention and result are opposite.

Application: This proverb comes from a Chinese classic story, and it is widely known to every Chinese family. The story unfolds like this: Once upon a time, there was a rich man, and this rich man possessed three hundred ounces of silver. However, the rich man was very concerned about his possession, and he worried that someone might steal his wealth away. One day, he decided to hide his three hundred ounces of silver in the ground.

The rich man did not want anyone to know where he buried his silver; therefore, he set a wooden board on the location where the treasure was. However, his heart was still full of anxiety, so he thought long and hard. All of a sudden, he came up with an idea of writing a sentence on the wooden board. He wrote, "There is no three hundred ounces of silver here." After all the work he did to secure his wealth, the rich man then went home with a perfectly undisturbed heart.

While the man was at home and immensely proud about what he did to his silver, the man's next-door neighbor was out wandering. He happened to spot the board; he removed the dirt and took the silver. The neighbor did not want anyone to know that he was the person who stole the silver, so he added a sentence on the wooden board. The sentence read, "Your next-door neighbor did not steal the silver."

You could laugh very hard about the two ridiculous individuals in the story. Nevertheless, the Chinese today use this proverb as a lesson. The lesson is: If the results of your actions are the opposite of what you expect, make a thorough examination of your intentions and actions.

Chinese proverb: da hai lao zhen.

大海捞针。

Translation: Try to find a needle in an ocean.

Meaning: It is a foolish thing to do.

Application: Every individual in this world knows that a needle is a very tiny object. If a person lost a tiny object in an enormous ocean, should that person make a huge endeavor to find it? The answer is no.

This proverb is a metaphor. The implication of this proverb is that people must value their recourses and be practical. If people indeed value their time and energy, then they will use them very effectively.

Chinese proverb: da zhi ruo yu.

大智若愚。

Translation: An intelligent person may pretend to be slow witted.

Meaning: Try to be modest.

Application: To try to be modest is the point of this proverb. According to Chinese philosophy, a modest person is like a bucket full of water. The bucket represents a person, and the water indicates knowledge. Although the bucket is full, it tries not to make any noise. Hence, a truly intelligent and modest person will be quiet or may even pretend to be slow-witted.

The Chinese also believe that the opposite is true. When a bucket is only half full of water, the bucket wants to make a lot noise. Those who do not actually possess much knowledge often like to brag about themselves.

If you are curious, you can perform an experiment of "testing for water noise". This experiment can be performed using the following steps:

1. Get two buckets of the same size and the same material.

2. Fill the first bucket with water completely full to the rim.

3. Fill the second bucket with only half full of water.

4. Then carry one on each of your hands and walk forward fast.

5. See which bucket will make more noise.

After the experiment, you should think about which bucket you would like to represent yourself. Would you like the half full bucket to represent you, or would you like the full bucket to represent you?

Chinese proverb: fei e tou huo.

飞蛾投火。

Translation: A moth darts into a flame willingly.

Meaning: One brings obliteration upon oneself.

Application: When a moth darts into a flame willingly, the consequence will be that the moth disappears completely. Why does a moth dart into the flame at its own will? Because it does not know any better. Then what does this proverb try to tell us? It tries to inform us that we should not destroy ourselves.

People are much more intelligent than moths; however, some individuals voluntarily get themselves into harmful situations.

If you have seen the movie *It's a Wonderful Life*, you might recall the scene in which George Bailey humbly begged Mr. Potter to lend him money. This is an example of someone trying to do an unwise thing in desperate circumstances.

Therefore, this proverb gives a warning to all individuals. If you are at the end of your rope, you must remind yourself that regardless of how dreadful the situation may be, you must think clearly to protect yourself.

Chinese proverb: hua qian yao hua zai dao kou shang.

花钱要花在刀口上。

Translation: Spend money shrewdly.

Meaning: Let people see your generosity and hide your frugality.

Application: This saying implies that if you are a frugal person, you need to spend your money very wisely. In other words, you need to let other people see your generosity and hide your frugality. If you are not a frugal person, then "Spend money shrewdly" is not applicable to you.

The following story will give you an idea of "Let people see your generosity and hide your frugality". A very close friend of mine was going to get married. The wedding was to be held at a faraway location. I really wanted to attend the wedding, however, I needed to figure out a couple of things before I could make up my mind. The first thing on my mind was the wedding gift, and the second thing was the purchasing of an airline ticket. I considered myself to be a frugal person, and I like to spend money very prudently. In other words, I wanted my friend think of me as a generous person, not as a stingy person.

After I had carefully weighed the possibilities, I decided not to attend the wedding. Instead of spending on the airline ticket, food, and hotel, I decided to be a blessing to my friend by giving him a $1200 wedding gift. The amount I did not spent on the traveling expenses allowed me to increase the wedding gift and still be frugal.

Chinese proverb: jiang cuo jiu cuo.

将错就错。

Translation: Leave a mistake uncorrected and make the best of it.

Meaning: Not every mistake can be corrected.

Application: We all make mistakes and not every mistake can be corrected. If a mistake is uncorrectable, the only thing that can be done is to make the best of it. How can we make the best of our mistakes? The following story gives an example of how this can be done.

Owen had a few close friends, and Paul was one of them. Paul wanted to invest in a business, which he believed would do very well. However, Paul did not have enough capital, so he encouraged his friends to either join him or lend the money to him. Owen loaned $20,000 to Paul as an investment. Unfortunately, Paul's business investments failed miserably, and he lost every penny of the investment.

The worst things in life sometimes come at a terrible time. Paul was in a dreadful financial condition, and he could not repay the $20,000 that he had borrowed from Owen. Therefore, it was not Paul but Owen who actually lost the money.

Owen realized that he had made a big mistake in lending money to Paul. $20,000 was a lot of money to Owen. Being generous and kind, Owen decided to forget the debt and remain friends with Paul. Furthermore, Owen considered himself a healthy person; he thought as long as he was healthy, he could always earn money.

Chinese proverb: jie ling hai xu ji ling ren.

解铃还须系铃人。

Translation: To untie the bell on the tiger requires the person who tied it.

Meaning: Whoever started the trouble should end the trouble.

Application: This proverb, which comes from the Ming dynasty, is based on an actual event. Because of its uniqueness, this event eventually became one of the recordings in the Ming dynasty. "Whoever started the trouble should end the trouble" can give you an idea of how to solve problems.

A very honorable Buddhist master resided in a monastery in Nanjing. At the same time, another Buddhist master also lived in that monastery. The second master was very candid; in addition to that, he did not want to be in charge. Because of these two facts, all monks in that monastery looked down at the second master. The only person who respected him was the honorable master.

One day, the honorable master was chatting with the monks. In the middle of chatting, he asked them a question. He said, "There is a tiger with a bell tied on its neck. Who can untie the bell for the tiger?" When the monks heard the question, they just stared at the honorable master. None of them could give an answer. At that moment, the second master happened to pass by and heard the question. At the request of the honorable master, he immediately answered, "The person who tied the bell on the tiger can untie the bell." The honorable master was very pleased with the answer. From that time on, none of the monks looked down at the second master any longer.

Today, the Chinese apply the concept of this proverb for solving problems. You may also think of this proverb when you need to resolve issues. According to the teaching of this proverb, the issue solver has to be the person who created the issue.

Chinese proverb: jin xin jin li.

尽心尽力。

Translation: One serves with all of one's heart and strength.

Meaning: A person gives truly the best effort.

Application: This proverb comes from one of the commentaries in Chinese history. A faithful servant who worked in the imperial palace during the Tang dynasty told the emperor that he would serve him with all of his heart and strength. His reason for doing this was to repay the kindness he had received from the emperor's late father.

This servant truly had a loyal heart toward the emperor. Although the actual event happened in the distant past, the principle is still applicable today. Loyalty is absolutely a value regardless of time; people today still need loyal friends.

Chinese proverb: jiu you zi qu.

咎由自取。

Translation: Bring calamity upon oneself.

Meaning: Have only oneself to blame.

Application: This proverb can also be sarcastically translated, "You get what you asked for." In a general sense, this proverb could pertain to a wide variety of calamities such as health problems, financial disasters, etc.

In my experience, I often see carefree individuals who are not concerned about the future bringing calamity upon themselves. Those people can be labeled as "rascals". Rascals know that what they seek to do is wrong and they do it anyway. In the end, they have no one to point their fingers to; instead, they have only themselves to blame.

Chinese proverb: li suo neng ji.

力所能及。

Translation: One can carry out a task within one's capability.

Meaning: Have the ability to achieve.

Application: Ever since my youth, I have made it a habit to observe individuals around me. Some of these individuals excelled academically; others excelled in different areas such as sewing, cooking, selling, etc.

Individuals who exceled academically often became teachers, researchers and doctors while people who possessed other capabilities worked as chefs, firefighters, hairdressers, etc. The important thing is that every person has an ability to achieve.

Chinese proverb: lie huo jian zhen jin.

烈火见真金。

Translation: The raging fire can test the purity of gold.

Meaning: Pure gold proves its worth in a blazing fire.

Application: A raging fire will not destroy gold, rather, it will refine and further purify the metal. Similarly, trials and troubles are like the raging fire in life, they test our true sturdiness. As we endure the testing, we refine and retain the spirit within us. Pure gold proves its worth in a blazing fire; we will be like gold and become much better and stronger people.

Chinese proverb: lin ji ying bian.

临机应变。

Translation: Change plans with any unforeseen event.

Meaning: Be prepared to modify plans.

Application: This proverb highlights the unwelcome but very common problem of having to change our plans due to unexpected events. Do unforeseen events happen often in reality? No one can give an accurate answer of how often this happens; however, it seems that life does not always go according to plan.

I would like to share the following story as an example: My friends, a couple, were preparing to retire. They decided that the husband should retire in a few years when he would reach the age of 67. Everything was going well until on the Friday morning of the husband's last day of work, he suddenly had a heart attack and passed away. That exact Friday was the day prior to the husband's 67th birthday. We were all sad at this event. The man's wife had to drastically change her plans.

Does the possibility of unforeseen events mean that we should not make any plans at all? No, it definitely does not! The proverb stresses flexibility. We need to keep planning and always be aware that the plan may have to change.

Chinese proverb: ke zhou qiu jian.

刻舟求剑。

Translation: Carve a mark on the boat to seek the sword.

Meaning: It is a wrong method.

Application: "Carve a mark on the boat to seek the sword" comes from a well-known Chinese story. The story is as follows: A certain man was crossing a river on a ferry boat. As the boat was moving along, the man accidentally dropped his precious sword into the river. The man believed that if he carved a mark on the side of the boat where his sword descended, he would find the sword. Therefore, he made his mark. After the boat arrived at its destination, the man began to search for his lost sword. He sought after his sword in the river based on the mark on the side of the boat. The man never found his sword.

The man used a wrong method to solve his problem. If he had used a correct approach, the chances of finding his sword would be increased. This proverb implies that we sometimes unintentionally apply wrong approaches for our problems. As we work to solve issues in life, we must choose a correct method; otherwise, we will receive disappointing results.

Chinese proverb: mao ku lao shu.

猫哭老鼠。

Translation: A cat weeps for a mouse.

Meaning: It is phony.

Application: Cats and mice are completely antagonistic, and they can never become friends. When a cat cries for a mouse, it is a false sympathy. Then what does this proverb try to tell us? This proverb suggests that our opponent is the "cat", and we are the "mouse".

If a cat shows kindness to a mouse, the mouse must be very alert. The kindness seen on the surface is only a covering for the perilous intention underneath. In other words, the compassion coming from our opponent is actually a cunning stratagem. When our cat weeps for us, we must watch out!

Chinese proverb: ming chui zhu bo.

名垂竹帛。

Translation: Renowned persons were recorded on bamboo and silk.

Meaning: History remembers famous individuals.

Application: China is well known for many inventions. Prominent among inventions in china are paper and gunpowder. In ancient China, prior to the invention of paper, bamboo and silk were used as the two primary materials to be written on. Chinese people used bamboo and silk for writing and for copying documents. Due to the fact that bamboo and silk were more expensive than the yet to be invented paper, the Chinese selected only the most important subjects to be written or to be copied. When the ancient Chinese recorded individuals' names on their bamboo or silk writing sheets, the intention was very clear. They wanted renowned individuals to be honored and remembered by future generations. In other words, recorded history was focused on helping us to remember prominent individuals.

We can apply the concept of this proverb by following two simple steps. The first step is to honor and remember well-known individuals. The second step is to learn from these historical individuals. In the midst of so many renowned individuals in Chinese history, Confucius stands out as a famous person. Along with other great individuals in Chinese history, we should study the life and accomplishments of Confucius.

Chinese proverb: pei le fu ren you zhe bing.

赔了夫人又折兵。

Translation: One lost not only a beauty but also soldiers.

Meaning: It is a double loss.

Application: This proverb comes from the famous Chinese historical novel named *Romance of The Three Kingdoms*. This novel centers on the power struggles of three kingdoms: Shu, Wei, and Wu. Shu wanted to remove the other two powers. Wei also had aggressive ambitions to take over Shu and Wu. On the same token, Wu wanted to be the only kingdom in China. Therefore, the emperors of these three kingdoms used all of the strategies they knew to eliminate the other two kingdoms and each emperor nearly exhausted all of his resources.

In the section of the novel where this proverb originates, one of the crafty stratagems of the emperor of Wu is described. This emperor wanted to remove the kingdom of Shu first, and then he would try to eliminate Wei.

The emperor of Wu used his own beautiful sister as bait to try to bring the emperor of Shu out where he would be killed. Instead of being killed, the emperor of Shu and the princess fell in love and were married.

Even though the princess just got married, her brother still wanted to kill her husband. The emperor of Shu, for saving himself, had to kill some of Wu's soldiers and escaped with his new wife. The strategy for eliminating Shu failed completely.

Chinese people today use this proverb to describe situations where a double loss has occurred.

Chinese proverb: tian you bu ce feng yun; ren you dan xi huo fu.

天有不测风云; 人有旦夕祸福。

Translation: A storm may arise from a clear sky; a person may meet a sudden event.

Meaning: Unexpected events can happen anytime.

Application: Weather is not always predictable, and ships have floundered when clear days turned into storms. Our lives, like the weather, can turn from normal into chaos in a matter of minutes. Unforeseeable events can happen at any moment.

We need to be mindful that while we very often receive great blessings, unhappy events can occur as well. There is one thing which we can do to help prevent unfortunate events from overtaking us. This very thing is to maintain a humble attitude. The storms of life often seem to be directed at the proud.

Chinese proverb: xing xing xi xing xing.

惺惺惜惺惺。

Translation: Intelligent people appreciate one another.

Meaning: Bright people understand each other.

Application: The first two and the last two characters of this proverb are the exactly same, the characters mean "intelligent people". The middle character implies "understanding" or "sympathetic". We can also translate the proverb as "Smart people understand one another."

When I think of this proverb, I think of the word "wise" as a deeper meaning for intelligent. A wise person often thinks deeper thoughts than imprudent people. Prudent people will search for hidden causes and seek answers to questions such as the meaning of life. Two wise people can understand, appreciate, and complement one another.

Chinese proverb: ye gong hao long.

叶公好龙。

Translation: Duke Ye loves dragons.

Meaning: Reality may not match what one claims.

Application: A very famous Chinese story is the source of this proverb.

Once there was a man who lived during the Spring and Autumn period in China. After the man's father passed away, he inherited his father's granted territory. Because the territory was located in Ye County, the man called himself Duke Ye. Duke Ye became widely known because he had a special passion for dragons.

Duke Ye loved dragons so much that they became the center of his life. Upon entering his house, images of dragons would make people's eyes dazzle. They could see dragons chiseled and carved on the walls, the pillars, and the ceiling.

The reputation of Duke Ye spread all over the land due to his excessive passion for dragons. The news of his affection for dragons even reached heaven. Hearing so much about Duke Ye's passion, a real dragon decided to come down from heaven to visit him. The real dragon was very anxious and he could hardly wait to meet Duke Ye in person.

Soon the day arrived! When the real dragon entered the house, Duke Ye looked up, and he was extremely horrified. Because of his totally dread of the real dragon, he immediately tried to take to his heels and escape. Unfortunately, Duke Ye could not even move an inch of his own body. His fear was so terrible that he fell entirely on the ground, and his soul left him.

This proverb points out that there are hypocrites in this world. If we desire to be sincere, then we must have our words and actions in accordance to our beliefs.

Chinese proverb: zhi tong dao he.

志同道合。

Translation: Cherish the same idea and follow the same path.

Meaning: Having a similar goal promotes success.

Application: Chinese people often say that two pairs of chopsticks are stronger than one pair. One pair can be broken easily; however, it is much harder to break two pairs of chopsticks.

As you work to become successful in life, you would be wise to find someone you know that has similar ideas and goals. Like the two pairs of chopsticks, a like-minded friend or partner can give more strength than one person alone. Two people often have more financial power, better ideas, and better support.

Chinese proverb: zhong gua de gua, zhong dou de dou.

种瓜得瓜, 种豆得豆。

Translation: Sow melon seeds get melons; sow bean seeds get beans.

Meaning: People reap what they planted.

Application: We reap what we sow. If we sow melon seeds, we will reap melons. If we plant beans, we will harvest beans. This is a law of nature, it cannot be any other way.

This law applies to our actions as well as to the planting of seeds. What we "sow" in our life will absolutely be what we harvest later on. If we "sow" seeds of kindness, we will receive kindness in return. If we "sow" seeds of malice, we will receive malice and hatred in return. The reaping may not occur right away, however, we will sooner or later receive our "harvest". We must always try to "sow" seeds of compassion and mercy. Sow compassion and get compassion; sow mercy and get mercy.

Chinese proverb: zi xi yu mao.

自惜羽毛。

Translation: Cherish one's own feather.

Meaning: Protect your name.

Application: "Cherish one's own feather" is a metaphor. Can you imagine a bird without its feathers? Such a bird would not only lose its ability to fly but also would look dreadful. Therefore, it is extremely important for the bird to protect its own feathers.

This proverb uses the word "feather" to indicate a person's reputation. Good reputations are difficult to obtain. They are built through years of respectable conduct and honest dealings with others. If we lose our good reputation, our creditability will suffer, and we then will be like birds without feathers. If we retain our honorable reputation through ethical conduct, our feathers will appear exceptionally radiant.

I believe that we undeniably need to cherish our own feathers. For this reason, I have placed this proverb as the last page of the book. My hope is that you will be able to use this proverb and all of the proverbs in this book as guidelines in your life.